Math in the Garden

Jennifer M. White
Katharine D. Barrett
Jaine Kopp
Christine Manoux
Katie Johnson
Yvette McCullough

Developed through a partnership of
University of California Botanical Garden and Lawrence Hall of Science
Berkeley, California

Published by KidsGardening
Burlington, Vermont

University of California Botanical Garden
200 Centennial Drive, Berkeley, CA 94720-5045
Director: Paul Licht

The University of California Botanical Garden at Berkeley is a living museum open to the public featuring one of the most diverse plant collections in the United States, and extensive education and outreach programs serving schools and community groups throughout California and the nation. Established in 1890, the Garden's 34 acres contain over 10,000 taxa and more than 20,000 accessions from all over the world arranged by region. The mission of the Garden is to develop and maintain a diverse living collection of plants to support teaching and worldwide research in plant biology, further the conservation of plant diversity, and promote public understanding and appreciation of plants and the natural environment. http://botanicalgarden.berkeley.edu

Lawrence Hall of Science
University of California
100 Centennial Drive, Berkeley, CA 94720-5200
Director: Dr. Rena Dorph

The Lawrence Hall of Science (LHS) is a public science center on the University of California at Berkeley campus. LHS offers a full program of activities for the public, including workshops and classes, exhibits, films, lectures, and special events. LHS is also a center for teacher education and curriculum research and development. Over the years, LHS educators have developed a multitude of curriculum guides, assembly programs, classes, and interactive exhibits. These successful programs are used widely throughout California, the nation, and the world by schools, science centers, museums, and community groups. http://lawrencehallofscience.org

Math in the Garden Program. The material is based upon work supported by the National Science Foundation under grant number ESI- 9909764. The Federal Government has certain rights in this material. Any opinions, findings, and conclusions or recommendations expressed in this material are those of the author(s) and do not necessarily reflect the views of the National Science Foundation.

HHMI

KidsGardening
132 Intervale Rd, Burlington, Vermont 05401
(802) 242-2748
Executive Director: Em Shipman

KidsGardening's mission is to create opportunities for kids to play, learn, and grow through gardening, engaging their natural curiosity and wonder. KidsGardening supports educators and families with grant funding, original educational resources, inspiration, and community to get more kids learning through the garden.

Copyright ©2006 by The Regents of the University of California. Published by the University of California and KidsGardening.org, Inc. All rights reserved.

ISBN-13: 978-0-9992234-8-2
Library of Congress Control Number: 2005937438

Project Staff

PROJECT DIRECTORS
Jennifer M. White
Katharine D. Barrett

NETWORK COORDINATOR
Christine Manoux

MATHEMATICS CURRICULUM SPECIALIST
Jaine Kopp

EXTERNAL EVALUATOR
Minda Borun

CURRICULUM SPECIALISTS
Katie Johnson
Yvette McCullough

COVER & ILLUSTRATIONS
Ann Williams

GRAPHIC DESIGN, LAYOUT & EDITING
Christine Manoux

CONTRIBUTING AUTHORS
José Franco
Jenny Maguire
Kimi Hosoume
Tim Aaronson
Esther Railton Rice

CONTRIBUTING ILLUSTRATORS
Lauri Twitchell

Jennifer M. White
Rose Craig
Katharine D. Barrett

CONTRIBUTING DESIGN & LAYOUT
Carl Babcock
Mike Horn
Shail Gala

ADVISORS
Beverly Braxton
Christine Boynton
Christopher Budd
Christopher Carmichael
Grace Coates

Robert Coulter
David Eisenbud
Lewis J. Feldman
Holly Forbes
Robert Gutowski
Leon Henkin
Robert Hyland
Robert Ornduff
Richard Ponzio
Cindy Reittinger
Hugo Rossi
Ellen Simms
Kathleen Socolofsky

Acknowledgements

Much as plant growth entails an interaction of numerous processes and resources, the development of this book has brought together the expertise of educators, youth leaders, parent volunteers, mathematicians, and scientists to engage children in using mathematics knowledge and skills to investigate garden environments. The following botanical gardens and museums played a central role in organizing and conducting the two national trials and summative evaluation with their informal education programs: Atlanta Botanical Garden, Brooklyn Botanic Garden, Brooklyn Children's Museum, Children's Museum of Houston, Missouri Botanical Garden, Morris Arboretum of the University of Pennsylvania, UC Botanical Garden, and UC Davis Arboretum.

A central goal of the project is to develop materials that are successful with diverse learners in non-school settings. The following youth and community programs were particularly helpful in arranging for materials to be trial-tested with their constituents: Berkeley Youth Alternative, Kids Breakfast Clubs of Hayward, Lazear Summer Garden Program, Malcolm X After-School Garden Club, Martin Luther King, Jr. Middle School Summer Garden Program, San Francisco Bay Area Girl Scout Council, California 4-H Youth Development Program, and West Contra Costa Integrated Waste Management Authority's Earth Day programs.

The Hayward Unified School District's Nutritional Learning Communities Program provided the leadership and support to trial test activities with parents and children in low-income neighborhoods. This feedback was crucial in helping to modify the activities so that concepts are age appropriate and accessible to diverse learners in weekend and after-school settings. The Orinda Union School District adopted *Math in the Garden* across all grades. Parent volunteers at every school made garden kits and supported the program being implemented in school and non-school sessions by the District Mathematics Specialist, Jenny Maguire.

Reviewers

We would like to thank the many individuals from around the nation who reviewed and tested the materials in manuscript and trial version form. Their critical comments and recommendations, based on presentation of these activities in informal settings, contributed significantly to this publication. Their role is an invaluable one, and their feedback is carefully recorded and integrated, as appropriate, into the publication. Their participation in the review process does not necessarily imply endorsement of *Math in the Garden* or responsibility for statements or views expressed in this publication.

Botanical Gardens

ATLANTA BOTANICAL GARDEN
Cindy Reittinger
Tracy McClendon
Mandy Horneber
Shannan LaPorte

BROOKLYN BOTANIC GARDEN
Robert Hyland
Sharon Myrie
Barbara Kushner-Kurland
Ted Maclin
Sonja Martin
Alexandra Chitty
Kelly Cole
Anthony Dedousis
Natalie Dhanoolal
Karenne Eng
Alyssa Gulino
Damali L'Elie
Allison Kruegar
Kym Libman
Tom Manual
Sharea Mines
Ruby Olisemeka
Argelis Rivera
Marilyn Sebro
Sybl Tate
Nekesha Williams

MISSOURI BOTANICAL GARDEN
Robert Coulter
Jennifer Hope
Peggy Kelly
Laura Schaefer

MORRIS ARBORETUM, PA
Robert Gutowski
Liza Hawley
Jane Alavi
Clare Brown
Joan Hanby
Sue Lake
Ruth McCard
Charlotte O'Donnell
Marcia Steinberg
Jim Traynor
Donna Wilhelm

UC BOTANICAL GARDEN
Christopher Carmichael
Holly Forbes
Ellen Simms

UC DAVIS ARBORETUM
Kathleen Socolofsky
Carmia Feldman
Betsy Faber
Megan Chiosso
Natalie Esparza
Bryn Feldman
Sara Kalmanovitz
Darius Paziradeh
Jonathan Quan
Anne Schellman
Laura Threlkeld
Naoki Yaya

Faculty Reviewers

UC BERKELEY INTEGRATIVE BIOLOGY
Robert Ornduff

UC BERKELEY PLANT PATHOLOGY
Lewis Feldman

UC BERKELEY MATHEMATICS
Leon Henkin

UC BERKELEY MATHEMATICAL SCIENCES RESEARCH INSTITUTE
David Eisenbud

UNIVERSITY OF BATH, ENGLAND, SCHOOL OF MATHEMATICAL SCIENCES
Christopher Budd

Science Museums

BROOKLYN CHILDREN'S MUSEUM
Nancy Cayemitte
Suzanne Tamang

CHILDREN'S MUSEUM OF HOUSTON
Karen Milnar
Rosa Henry
Felicia Johnson
Aisha Lewis
Christina Loanzo
Misty Miller
Margaret Robert
Angie Saenz
Kyra Stevens
Asenat Treviño
Hifa Ungamootoo
Mary Williams

MANGINI AGRICULTURAL MUSEUM
Marisa Neelon

Youth Programs

BERKELEY YOUTH ALTERNATIVE
Danny Engleberg

EAST BAY CONSERVATION CORPS
Fiona Tavernier
Moira Chapman

SAN FRANCISCO BAY AREA GIRL SCOUTS COUNCIL
Jean Fahy
Pam Webster

CA 4-H YOUTH DEVELOPMENT
Richard Ponzio
Dan Desmond
Ramona Carlos
Carol Martin (El Dorado County)
Jeannette George (Tehama County)
Bret Corzine
Lynne Elrick
Barbara Foudy
Jennifer Kochishan
Susan Langhlin
Jann Leverenz
Sandy Martin
Kevin Martin
Sherrie Taylor
Jason Zakem
Lisa Zane

Informal Programs

MARTIN LUTHER KING, JR, MIDDLE SCHOOL, CA
Neil Smith
Beth Sonnenberg

CRESTMONT ELEMENTARY SCHOOL, CA
Susan Danek
Susan Weiner

ENCINAL ELEMENTARY, CA
Ruth Peterson

LAZEAR ELEMENTARY, CA
Sonya Rodriquez

MALCOLM X ELEMENTARY, CA
Rivka Mason

MARKHAM ELEMENTARY, CA
Jessica Harr, Cecilia Jun
Darolyn Lew
Melinda Cespedes

MELROSE ELEMENTARY, CA
Laura Pesavento

PARK ELEMENTARY, CA
Becky Bear

SHILLING ELEMENTARY, CA
Cindy Chinn

SLATER ELEMENTARY, CA
Carmen Bryant
Helen Choy
Lee Ann Wilson

ST. JEROME SCHOOL, CA
Mary Jo Mishork

ST. PERPETUA SCHOOL, CA
Theresa Slaman

HOME SCHOOL PARENTS
Diane Keith
Michelle Boyd
Wendi Fawns
Amy Pleatman
Andrea Veltman

KENNEDY MONTESSORI, KY
Kaki Robinson

CASITA CENTER, CA
Lou Ann Countryman

Table of Contents

INTRODUCTION 7
    Activity Format 8
    Math/Science Standards and Age chart 10
    Making a Garden Journal 12

CHAPTER ONE — NUMBER, OPERATIONS, & ALGEBRA 13
    How Many Seeds in a Tomato? 15
    Everything Counts in the Garden 19
    Locating Garden Treasures 23
    Inside the Coordinate Grid 27
    Comparing the Area of Leaves 31
    Area & Perimeter of Leaves 35
    Half of a Half of My Garden Plot 39
    Ratios of Shoots and Roots 43
    Soil + Water Profile 47

CHAPTER TWO — MEASUREMENT 51
    Hand Spans 52
    Centimeter by Centimeter 56
    Garden Harvest — Measuring Length 60
    Plant Study — Measuring Growth 64
    Measuring with Steps 68
    How Much Space Does It Take? 71
    Mud Shakes 75
    Weighing the Garden Harvest 79

MATH IN THE GARDEN

CHAPTER THREE — GEOMETRY & PATTERN 83

- "Geometric Shapes" Chart 84
- Cross Cut Snacks 86
- Shapes in the Garden 90
- The Great Triangle Hunt 93
- Geometric Windows 97
- Angle Search 101
- Planting in Circles 105
- Pattern Snacks 110
- Symmetry — Find That Line 114
- Symmetry Inside Fruit 118
- Drawing Tree Observations 122

CHAPTER FOUR — DATA ANALYSIS 126

- Data Snacks 127
- Leaf Attributes 131
- Flowers: Graph & Graph Again 135
- What's in Garden Soil? 139
- Plant Predators — Sampling Evidence 144
- Bud, Flower, Fruit Data 148
- Self-Similarity 153
- Shadows — Change Over Time 157

Introduction

Gardens are magical settings filled with colorful shapes, delightful aromas, and myriad patterns that excite the imagination and awaken the senses. As people of all ages plant, harvest, and relax in gardens, they are enlivened by the unexpected discoveries of a new blossom, a bountiful harvest of fruit, and an emerging butterfly. The hidden treasure in gardens is math.

Patterns, measurement, comparisons, and problem solving are a few of the mathematics strands embedded in typical gardening activities. The University of California Botanical Garden, in collaboration with the Lawrence Hall of Science, has developed engaging math activities that anyone can do. Math in the Garden takes you on an exploration of the garden using a mathematical lens through which adults and children alike discover a joy in honing math skills as they investigate soil, shadows, fruits, and flowers.

Funded by the National Science Foundation in 1999, and supported in part by the Howard Hughes Medical Institute, the Math in the Garden activities have been extensively trial-tested across the country. After-school youth leaders and educators from botanical gardens, garden clubs, community youth groups, 4-H programs, Girl Scouts, Boy Scouts, summer camps, home-schooling groups, parent volunteers, and classroom teachers have taught the investigations and contributed their insights.

Math in the Garden provides support for teaching national math and science standards. The lessons are grouped into 4 mathematical thematic categories: Numbers, Operations and Algebra, Measurement, Geometry and Patterns, and Data Analysis. They are connected to the science domains of Earth and Space Science, Life Science, Physical Science and Engineering, Technology and Applications of Science. A key linking lesson content to specific math and science categories can be found on page 10 and 11. The activities within each lesson are also designed to promote inquiry, language arts, and nutrition.

Each delightfully illustrated investigation has an easy-to-follow format and can be completed within an hour. The inexpensive equipment and materials necessary for the activities can be found in most homes and garden programs. The format and rationale for various elements of an activity are displayed on the following pages.

We hope you enjoy your adventures using Math in the Garden.

Activity Format

A lightning bug icon illuminates math concepts and skills featured in the activity.

This denotes the **age range** for which this activity best matches the math standards and math thinking of children and youth, and reflects the diversity of mathematical abilities found within groups of children. In any given age range, older children often can take the math analysis deeper.

Charts and tables, as well as homemade tools, are listed in the **What You Need** section. Instructions on how to make them are included in the **Getting Ready** section.

Group Size: Most activities are designed for children to work with a partner to promote shared ideas and observations. In all cases, however, children should journal their own findings and take turns with tasks. If you are working with just a few children, have them collect additional sets of information to make the analysis of data more interesting. Become a child's partner, if working with only one child, and encourage her to take the lead in collecting and analyzing data.

Children are encouraged, whenever practical, to record their observations, data, and ideas in their **journals** to promote language development, recording skills, and reflective thinking. Keeping data like a field biologist allows children to make comparisons over time that lead to new explorations and "ahas." When children make their own journals they use them more. A simple way to make a garden journal is described on page 12.

The garden is a wonderful, large space to explore. **Numberlines and grid lines** that are made for several of the activities in Chapter 1 are convenient, long measuring tools that can be used again and again in other investigations.

This **flower icon** (✽) identifies questions to use with children. These questions have been designed to promote math conversations and thinking, and to stimulate the application of mathematics to new situations. Open-ended questions that have no single right answer are used periodically to stimulate children's ideas. In the spirit of how scientists share their thinking, welcome diverse answers from youth. Go on to explain why you will have them use a specific approach or method, providing a brief rationale. Brackets following questions contain examples of possible answers.

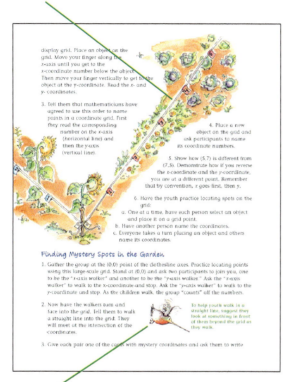

A **hummingbird icon** points out helpful notes for success in conducting the activities.

A **databoard** can be made from a piece of thick cardboard, ledger-sized paper (11" x 17") and medium-sized binder clips. Use this handy display tool out of doors to provide a flat surface to sort objects, outline procedures, illustrate math concepts, model techniques of recording, and give children practice in presenting data.

More Math in the Garden provides additional activity ideas that build upon, and enrich, the mathematical experiences and concepts presented in the main activity.

MATH IN THE GARDEN

MATH CONTENT KEY ● = Key Content • = Additional Content	MATH CONCEPTS				for Ages								
Math in the Garden	Number, Operations & Algebra	Measurement	Geometry & Pattern	Data Analysis									
Page / Activity					5	6	7	8	9	10	11	12	13
56 / Centimeter by Centimeter	•	●			▓	▓	▓	▓					
31 / Comparing the Area of Leaves	●		•		▓	▓	▓	▓					
122 / Drawing Tree Observations		•	●		▓	▓	▓	▓					
19 / Everything Counts in the Garden	●				▓	▓	▓	▓					
97 / Geometric Windows			●	•	▓	▓	▓	▓					
23 / Locating Garden Treasures	●				▓	▓	▓	▓					
75 / Mud Shakes		●		•	▓	▓	▓	▓					
90 / Shapes in the Garden			●		▓	▓	▓	▓					
86 / Cross Cut Snacks			●	•	▓	▓	▓	▓					
127 / Data Snacks				●	▓	▓	▓	▓					
135 / Flowers: Graph & Graph Again	•			●	▓	▓	▓	▓					
60 / Garden Harvest — Measuring Length		●		•	▓	▓	▓	▓					
93 / The Great Triangle Hunt		•	●		▓	▓	▓	▓					
52 / Hand Spans		●		•	▓	▓	▓	▓					
15 / How Many Seeds in a Tomato?	●				▓	▓	▓	▓					
71 / How Much Space Does it Take?		●	•	•	▓	▓	▓	▓					
131 / Leaf Attributes				●	▓	▓	▓	▓					
68 / Measuring with Steps		●			▓	▓	▓	▓					
110 / Pattern Snacks			●		▓	▓	▓	▓					
144 / Plant Predators — Sampling Evidence				●	▓	▓	▓	▓					
114 / Symmetry — Find That Line			●		▓	▓	▓	▓					
118 / Symmetry Inside Fruit			●		▓	▓	▓	▓					
139 / What's in Garden Soil?				●	▓	▓	▓	▓					
79 / Weighing the Garden Harvest		●			▓	▓	▓	▓					
101 / Angle Search		•	●					▓	▓	▓	▓	▓	▓
35 / Area & Perimeter of Leaves	●		•	•				▓	▓	▓	▓	▓	▓
148 / Bud, Flower, Fruit Data				●				▓	▓	▓	▓	▓	▓
39 / Half of a Half of My Garden Plot	●							▓	▓	▓	▓	▓	▓
27 / Inside the Coordinate Grid	●							▓	▓	▓	▓	▓	▓
105 / Planting in Circles			●					▓	▓	▓	▓	▓	▓
64 / Plant Study — Measuring Growth		●		•				▓	▓	▓	▓	▓	▓
43 / Ratios of Shoots and Roots	●			•				▓	▓	▓	▓	▓	▓
153 / Self-Similarity			•	●				▓	▓	▓	▓	▓	▓
157 / Shadows — Change Over Time		•		●				▓	▓	▓	▓	▓	▓
47 / Soil + Water Profile	●	•		•				▓	▓	▓	▓	▓	▓

Physical Science	Life Science	Earth & Space Science	Engineering, Technology and Applications of Science	Math in the Garden Activity
	●		●	Centimeter by Centimeter
	●		●	Comparing the Area of Leaves
	●		●	Draw Tree Observations
				Everything Counts in the Garden
			●	Geometric Windows
			●	Locating Garden Treasures
●		●	●	Mud Shakes
			●	Shapes in the Garden
	●		●	Cross Cut Snacks
			●	Data Snacks
	●		●	Flowers: Graph and Graph Again
	●		●	Garden Harvest — Measuring Length
			●	Great Triangle Hunt
			●	Hand Spans
	●		●	How Many Seeds in a Tomato?
●			●	How Much Space Does it Take?
	●		●	Leaf Attributes
			●	Measuring with Steps
	●		●	Pattern Snacks
	●		●	Plant Predators — Sampling Evidence
	●			Symmetry — Find That Line
	●			Symmetry Inside Fruit
●		●	●	What's in Garden Soil?
●			●	Weighing the Garden Harvest
			●	Angle Search
			●	Area & Perimeter of Leaves
	●		●	Bud, Flower, Fruit Data
			●	Half of a Half of My Garden Plot
			●	Inside the Coordinate Grid
			●	Planting in Circles
	●		●	Plant Study — Measuring Growth
	●		●	Ratios of Shoots and Roots
	●		●	Self-Similarity
●			●	Shadows — Change Over Time
●		●	●	Soil + Water Profile

Making a Garden Journal

In these Math in the Garden activities, children and youth use a journal to record data, draw observations, and write their reflections about experiences in the garden. This is a simple, attractive way to create a journal to document garden explorations.

Place about 10 sheets of **paper** (5½" x 8½" is a great size) on top of a piece of the same size of **cardstock.** You can put a **cover** on top of it, but it must be flexible enough to flip over to the back.

Punch two **holes** at the top of the paper and cardstock about one inch from each side. From the backside, thread a medium-sized **rubber band** through one hole. Loop it around one end of a **stick** on the front side. Thread the other end of the rubber band through the second hole and fasten it around the other end of the stick.

Decorate the cover. Handy tools to draw on the backside of the journal's edge are a 6-inch ruler along one side and a 15-centimeter ruler along the other.

CHAPTER ONE
Number, Operations, & Algebra

Mathematics helps us describe the world around us. The garden lends itself to explorations of number, operation and algebra activities — from simple counting and tallying of objects found in the garden to estimating the number of seeds in a tomato to determining the ratios of shoots and roots. Algebraic concepts are also tied in through use of a life-size coordinate grid and by dividing garden plots into fractional parts.

Numbers are quantifiers — in counting they tell us "how many" and in measuring, "how much." Since numbers permeate all of mathematics, as well as our daily lives, children need to gain an understanding of numbers — what they represent and how they are used.

The "counting numbers" {1, 2, 3, 4 …} are the very first numbers that we learn. When a zero is added, it becomes the set of whole numbers {0, 1, 2, 3, 4…}. In using the digits from 0 to 9, it is possible to represent any number in our base ten system.

Children begin to learn about numbers through concrete, real world experiences. They count objects of interest, such as the number of petals on a flower. Numbers are also used to measure in units, such as feet, as in "how many feet tall is your sunflower?" and to make comparisons, such as "which sunflower is tallest?"

Estimation is a useful life skill that helps us gauge a quantity without counting precisely. As children have opportunities to estimate, they gain deeper number sense about the magnitude of numbers and measures. Estimation skills help assess the reasonableness of an answer. It is important not to turn estimation into a contest when it is used as a learning tool in mathematics.

The four basic operations — addition, subtraction, multiplication, and division — are the first things most people think of when they hear the word "math." Although mathematics involves more than these computational operations, computational skills are the

MATH IN THE GARDEN

foundation for problem solving and higher mathematics, such as algebra, geometry, and statistics. Children need these computational tools in order to acquire fluency with number facts. The activities in this section provide opportunities to practice and further develop computational skills.

Algebra is often called the language of mathematics. The language includes digits (0...9), letters (variables/unknowns), operation symbols (+ addition, − subtraction, x multiplication, and ÷ division) relations symbols (= equal, ≠ not equal, > greater than, < less than, ≥ greater than or equal to, ≤ less than or equal to), and punctuation, such as parentheses. These symbols and notations are used to write mathematical statements.

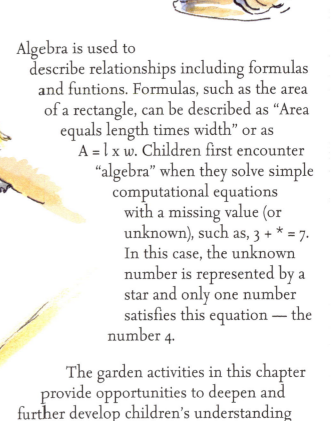

Algebra is used to describe relationships including formulas and funtions. Formulas, such as the area of a rectangle, can be described as "Area equals length times width" or as $A = l \times w$. Children first encounter "algebra" when they solve simple computational equations with a missing value (or unknown), such as, $3 + * = 7$. In this case, the unknown number is represented by a star and only one number satisfies this equation — the number 4.

The garden activities in this chapter provide opportunities to deepen and further develop children's understanding of numbers and how they are used to quantify (how many) and quaify (how much) the things around them.

How Many Seeds in a Tomato?

Ages 5-13

This activity engages estimation and counting skills.

Youth develop and practice estimation skills as they cut open tomatoes and count the seeds. They then estimate how many tomatoes can be grown from the seeds of one tomato.

What You Need

For Each Pair
- cutting board
- serrated plastic knife
- 8 cherry or 'Sweet 100' tomatoes
- 2 additional larger tomatoes
- 6-inch string, ribbon, or paper strip
- flat toothpicks
- ruler
- journals
- pencils and crayons

Getting Ready

1. Identify a picnic table or flat area of the garden where pairs of children can dissect their tomatoes.

2. Purchase several dozen small cherry tomatoes as well as a variety of larger tomatoes so there are enough for each person to taste as well as dissect.

3. Cut 6-inch lengths of string or strips of paper to serve as measuring tools, and assemble the materials.

MATH IN THE GARDEN

Here We Go

1. Give each child a few small cherry tomatoes to eat as a snack. Ask:
   - How many seeds do you think are inside each tomato?
   - Do you think each tomato has the same number of seeds?

2. Tell them they can estimate the number of seeds inside a tomato without opening it!

3. Ask the youth how they would determine if two tomatoes are the same size. They may say, "having a similar distance around" — the same circumference.

4. Accept their suggestions and then demonstrate how to use string or a strip of paper to estimate the circumference of a tomato.

5. Pair the children and direct them to choose a method to determine if tomatoes are the same size. They can measure the circumference, eyeball it, measure the height, and so on.

Estimating How Many Seeds in a Small Tomato

1. Give youth a flexible measuring tool such as string, and have them select 4 tomatoes of similar size. Ask them to use their size-determining method to compare their tomatoes.

2. Give each pair a cutting board, toothpicks, journals, crayons, and pencils. Have the youth examine their tomatoes, and then draw the tomato's actual size.

3. Before cutting open the tomato, have each pair estimate the number of seeds inside. Tell children that it is okay, and expected, that their estimations do not exactly match the actual number of seeds. As they practice and gather more data, their estimations will get closer to the actual amounts. Have them write their estimations next to their drawing. Put a big "E" next to it to note it is an estimation of the number of seeds.

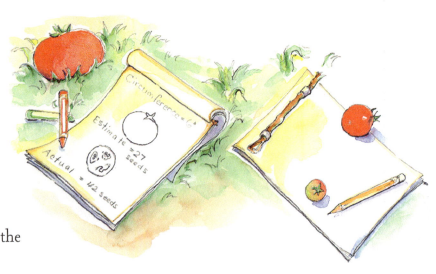

4. Have each pair cut one tomato in half. Demonstrate how to use the plastic knife. Depending upon the skills of your students, give each pair a knife or have them show you where they will make one cut. Give them the knife and then retrieve it.

5. Have each child count the seeds in one half of the tomato using the toothpicks to separate the seeds from the "jelly." Encourage them to look closely. Ask:
    ❀ Are the seeds all the same size?
    ❀ Do any seeds look dead? How many?
    ❀ What is the purpose of the jelly around the seeds? [protection]
    Discuss ways of counting large numbers of seeds. [grouping into 5s or 10s, counting half and adding together]

6. Tell the youth to add together the numbers of seeds they counted in each half and record that total next to their estimation. Put an "A" by it for actual.

Comparing Tomatoes

1. Have the children repeat the steps above for each remaining tomato, always making an estimate first. Ask:
    ❀ Is the number of seeds the same in all tomatoes that are the same size?
    ❀ If not, how close are the numbers of seeds?
    ❀ What was the largest number of seeds you found? Smallest?
    ❀ What is the range of the number of seeds? [range = highest number minus the lowest number]
    ❀ What is the average number of seeds? [total number of seeds for all tomatoes divided by number of tomatoes]
    ❀ Did your estimation change as you opened more tomatoes?
    ❀ How did your estimation change?

MATH IN THE GARDEN

2. Hold up a tomato and ask how many seeds they estimate are inside. If they feel confident they "know" the number of seeds, do not cut open the tomato. By now, children often feel confident they can estimate the number of seeds. If they are unsure, open the tomato and count the seeds together.

Estimating How Many Seeds in Large Tomatoes

1. Hold up a large tomato and ask how many tomato plants can grow from one tomato. Give each pair a large tomato. Have the youth estimate its number of seeds. Ask questions, such as:
   ❋ How did they make this estimation?
   ❋ Will there be more seeds than in their smaller tomatoes?
   ❋ Will the seeds be larger?

2. Have the children draw the large tomato in their journal, then cut it open and look at the seeds. Ask:
   ❋ Do you want to revise your estimate?
   ❋ Are the seeds bigger or smaller in this tomato?
   ❋ How many dead seeds do you estimate there are?

3. Have the youth subtract the number of dead seeds from their estimate. This answer is their estimate for the number of seeds that could produce a new tomato plant. Have them record this number in their journal.

4. Have the youth count and record the actual number of seeds. Ask:
   ❋ How does the number of seeds in the large tomato compare to the number of seeds in the small tomato?
   ❋ Does the size of a tomato help you estimate the number of seeds? Why or why not?

More Math in the Garden

Estimation Challenge Have children challenge each other in estimating the number of seeds in different tomatoes. Ask: "What helps make an estimate close to the actual number?" Invite the youth to share their strategies.

Estimation Comparison Have youth compare different varieties of tomatoes, such as heirlooms. Look at size, shape, and quantity of seeds. Ask: "How does the number of seeds in the different varieties compare?"

Everything Counts in the Garden

Ages 5-8

This activity explores number sense, tally, and number sequence.

Children develop a one-to-one correspondence of number and object while they count items found in the garden. They tally the number of interesting things they find and "walk" those numbers on a giant numberline.

What You Need

For Each Child
- 3" x 5" index card
- pencil and crayons

For the Group
- plastic clothesline, 25 feet
- roll of 2-inch-wide plastic tape
- wide-tipped black permanent pen
- extra 3" x 5" index cards

Getting Ready

1. Using a plastic clothesline, make a numberline beginning with zero and numbered at 1-foot intervals through 20 using 6-inch strips of the plastic tape folded over the line to label with numbers. Leave extra line beyond the 20 mark, so tallies may be placed in a

MATH IN THE GARDEN

"larger than 20" category on the numberline. Have the line ready and available in the garden to use after the children have tallied their objects.

2. Visit the garden ahead of time to note any "off limit" counting areas, and to identify an easily visible object to use as an example. Choose something like trees that number more than five and fewer than 10, so that you can demonstrate the tally process.

Here We Go

1. Gather the children as a group and ask them what types of things they might find in the garden. [plants, flowers, garden tools, stumps, rocks, insects, birds, butterflies, snails]

2. Ask their ideas for ways to count various living and non-living objects. [count on fingers, make tally marks] How might they count and keep track of animals like birds that are moving around in the garden? [Notice distinctive individual markings, and make a mark for each new individual.]

3. Explain that they will choose an item to count, and draw it on an index card. Model how to draw, count, and tally a sample item such as trees. Encourage children to choose different objects so that the group learns about a large variety of things in a garden.

4. Distribute the index cards, and have children draw the item they will be counting. Review how to make tally marks, and check that the children understand the marks and meaning of a tally.

5. Send them into the garden to conduct their counts.

Counting and Recording

1. Circulate among the children, checking that they are associating one tally mark with one object.

2. Ask counting questions while they are working, such as:
   ❀ How many do you have in your tally?
   ❀ How do you count objects that appear in a group?
   ❀ Where did you find most of the objects you counted?
   ❀ Where did you find the least?
   ❀ What method will you use to check your counting?

Walking the Numberline

1. Gather children where you have positioned the numberline, and have them sit or stand with the numberline in view.

2. Ask them to look at the numberline and describe what they see. [It has numbers; it is a line; it starts with zero; there are spaces between the numbers; it has numbers that go up to 20.]

Children need this time to examine and talk about the numberline to make the connection between the tallies and the numerical representations.

3. Tell children they will use this numberline to place their cards at the number that matches the number of the objects they counted. Ask them how many giraffes are in the garden. When they answer "none" or "zero," sketch a giraffe and place the card at the zero point of the numberline.

4. Using the card you made with the group at the beginning of the activity, have children count the tally marks with you. Model how to start at "0," counting off marks as you step from number to number along the line, until you arrive at the number represented by the tally marks. Place the card on the ground below the number.

5. Ask a child to stand at zero with her index card. "What object was counted?" Have her walk the number of the tally marks and place her card below that number. [2 butterflies will have a tally of 2, and the card will be placed below the number 2.] Repeat until all children have placed their cards along the numberline. If more than one object has the same tally, arrange the cards, one below the other, at the designated number.

6. If you have a small group, have children repeat the activity and count a new object to add to the array of garden objects.

Using the Numberline

1. Have the children examine the numberline. Ask:
   ❀ Which object has the greatest count?
   ❀ Which object has the least count?
   ❀ Did any objects have the same tally?
   ❀ How does the numberline help us?

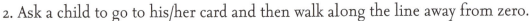

2. Ask a child to go to his/her card and then walk along the line away from zero.
   ❀ Do the numbers get smaller or bigger?

   Ask another child to walk from his/her card towards the zero.
   ❀ Do the numbers get bigger or smaller?

More Math in the Garden

Numberline Stroll Gather the cards from the numberline; shuffle and distribute cards to the children. Have them walk the numberline according to the tally marks on their cards and place their cards on the line.

A Second Census Conduct a second counting survey on another day using cards that are colored differently from the ones used for the first tally. Have children compare the results of their two tallies by placing the cards on the numberline. Guide them in determining which objects, after the second tally, have more individuals (How many more?), which have remained the same, and which have fewer numbers (How many less?).

Locating Garden Treasures

Ages 5-8

Children locate "treasures" in the garden using a life-sized coordinate grid. They plot the coordinates for items, such as sunflowers, water faucets, pumpkins, and mulberry trees.

This grid uses both letters (for x-axis) and numbers (for y-axis) to learn the conventions of graphing on a coordinate grid.

What You Need

For Each Pair
- several 3" x 5" index cards
- pencils and crayons

For the Group
- 2 plastic clotheslines, at least 12 meters each
- 2 colors of rolls of 2-inch-wide plastic tape
- wide-tipped black permanent pen
- databoard
- 2 sheets of 1-inch-squared graph paper
- 2 colors of marking pens (same colors as tape)
- several tall stakes
- meter stick

MATH IN THE GARDEN

Getting Ready

1. Leaving enough line at the ends to tie them to garden structures, tape one clothesline at 1-meter intervals with one color of tape. Use the wide-tipped pen to label the tape, beginning with a zero and continuing with alphabetical letters A through J. This will represent the x-axis of the life-sized grid. Use the other color of tape to label the second line, which will be your y-axis. Begin with zero and at 1-meter intervals continue through 10.

2. Draw and label two identical coordinate grids on each sheet of graph paper. Label the x-axis beginning with zero, then A through J, with a pen the same color as the tape of the letter rope. Label the y-axis in the same color as the tape of the numberline. One of these grids will become your secret "master grid" for the "treasure" hunt. On the other grid, children will record the coordinates and drawings of the objects that they locate in the garden.

3. In the garden, tie the two lines about 2 feet above the ground to the same object so that the zeros overlap. Extend the lines to form a 90° angle. Standing with your back to the (0,0) location, the lettered x-axis is on your right and the numbered y-axis is on your left. As needed, use garden structures and stakes to keep the lines straight and off the ground to be easily seen.

4. With the master grid and pencil in hand, walk into the life-sized grid and record about 20 garden objects for the children to locate (birdbath, sunflower, stepping stone, water faucet, corn stalk). Write the coordinates and objects on the master grid with the x-coordinate first, followed by the y-coordinate, for example, (C,4).

5. Write each set of coordinates on a separate 3" x 5" index card. Don't name the object! The children will use the coordinates to locate and identify the objects. Cover the master grid with the blank one, which will be used with the children.

Here We Go

1. Gather the children near the (0,0) point of the garden grid, and tell them they will use this giant grid, which is similar to a map, to locate garden "treasures." Ask:
   ❀ What treasures might we find in our garden? [flowers, tomatoes, insect egg cases, bird feeders, seedlings, benches]

2. Show the group the blank coordinate grid attached to the databoard. Ask:
   ❀ What do you notice about this grid?
   Be sure to note that one line, or "axis," has letters, and the other axis has numbers. Have them locate where the two axes meet at (0,0), just like the giant grid. This point (0,0) is the starting point, the grid's point of origin.

3. Tell children that mathematicians have agreed on a way to name points in a grid. First they read the letter or number on the horizontal line, and then the number or letter on vertical line. This system is used for mapping.

4. Pick one card of coordinates to demonstrate how to locate a point using the databoard grid, for example (C,4). Start at (0,0) and use your fingers to "walk" along the alphabet line, 0 to A to B, stopping at C. With the other hand, have your fingers "walk" from 0 to 1 to 2 to 3, stopping at 4.

5. Ask a child to point to where the two lines will intersect if you "walk" your fingers straight out into the grid along the imaginary vertical "C-line" and the imaginary horizontal "4-line." Circle the point with a colored marker.

6. Choose another card and have new volunteers help you locate the new spot.

Walking the Garden Grid

1. Familiarize children with the life-size coordinate grid. Stand at (0,0) and ask two participants to join you, one to be the "letter-walker" and another to be the "number-walker."

2. Ask the letter-walker to walk along the x-axis to the letter C and stop. Ask the number-walker to walk along the y-axis to the number 4 and stop. As the children walk, the group "counts" off the letters and numbers.

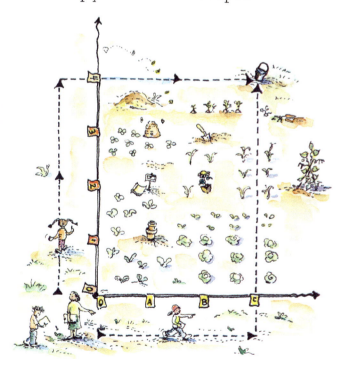

MATH IN THE GARDEN

3. Have the letter-walker and the number-walker turn and face into the grid. Tell the letter-walker to move away from the x-axis and into the grid in a straight line and the number-walker to move away from the y-axis and into the grid in a straight line. They will meet at the intersection of the "C-line" and the "4-line," which is (C,4). Ask: "What treasure did you find?" Have them draw or write the object on the card.

To help children walk in a straight line, suggest they look at something directly in front of them beyond the grid as they walk.

4. Give another card to a new pair of volunteers and have them demonstrate how to locate and draw the new object.

Locating the Treasures

1. Distribute two prepared cards and a pencil to each pair and have the children work together using the coordinates to locate and identify the two garden objects. When they have located and drawn the two "treasures," have them return to the databoard and draw or write the names of the objects at the corresponding location on the paper grid.

2. As the coordinates of the cards get identified and the objects recorded on the databoard grid, recirculate the index cards and have the children check the findings of the other pairs. You can check for accuracy by looking at your "master grid" and assist the pairs as needed.

3. Gather the group to view the databoard grid. By now the grid should have a dozen or more objects plotted and drawn. Congratulate the children for having created a map of items in the garden.

4. Pose reflective questions, such as:
   ❧ How would you record the location of new objects?
   ❧ What kinds of people use coordinate grids in their jobs? [surveyors, artists, architects]
   ❧ What else could you make a coordinate map for? [making a mural, playing a game, mapping your bedroom]

More Math in the Garden

Enriching the Garden Map Have children further develop the map of the garden by identifying more features and objects in the garden to plot and draw on the databoard grid.

Garden Treasure Hunt Children make up their own lists of coordinates linked to mystery garden objects for other pairs to locate and draw.

Inside the Coordinate Grid

Ages 8-13

This activity introduces an x- and y-coordinate grid and graphing language to locate points in the garden.

Youth use coordinates in a life-sized grid to find locations of items in the garden. They then place stakes in the garden grid and record the coordinates for others to find.

What You Need

For Each Pair
- 3" x 5" index card
- pencil

For the Group
- 2 plastic clotheslines, at least 12 meters each
- 2 colors of rolls of 2-inch-wide plastic tape
- wide-tipped black permanent pen
- databoard
  – 2 sheets of 1-inch-squared graph paper
- 2 colors of marking pens (same colors as tape)
- small tokens (such as pebbles, acorns, pennies)
- several tall stakes
- meter stick
- craft sticks

MATH IN THE GARDEN

Getting Ready

1. Make two grid axes from the clotheslines. Leave enough line at the ends to tie them to garden structures. Place pieces of plastic tape numbered at 1-meter intervals on each of the lines. Start numbering with a zero and continue through 10. Use a different color tape for each line — one for the x-axis and one for the y-axis.

2. On each sheet of graph paper, draw and label a coordinate grid with numbered x-axis and y-axis. Use the pen color that matches the axis color of the clothesline. One grid will be your "master" with locations, and the other will be a display grid used with the youth.

3. In the garden, tie the two numbered lines about 2 feet above the ground to the same object so that the zeros overlap. Extend the numbered lines to form a 90° angle. Standing with your back to the (0,0) location, the x-axis is on your right, and the y-axis is on your left. As needed, use garden structures and stakes to keep the lines straight and off the ground to be easily seen.

4. Choose about 10 objects in the garden that cannot move and are inside your x- and y-axis lines. Make a key for the activity by recording these objects with their coordinates on the master grid with the x coordinate first, followed by the y coordinate (x,y).

5. For each pair of youth, make a card with the coordinate locations of at least 5 of these mystery objects. Sequence them differently on each card. This way each pair starts at a different place in the garden.

Here We Go

1. Out in the garden, gather around the databoard. Find out what the group knows about coordinate grids. Ask:
   ❀ Who has seen or used a grid like this before? For what purpose?
   ❀ Where is the x-axis? [It's the horizontal number line across the bottom.]
   ❀ Where is the y-axis? [It's the vertical number line up the side.]
   ❀ Where is the origin point? [at (0,0)]

2. Demonstrate how to use coordinate numbers to locate a specific point on the display

MATH IN THE GARDEN

grid. Place an object on the grid. Move your finger along the x-axis until you get to the x-coordinate number below the object. Then move your finger vertically to get to the object at the y-coordinate. Read the x- and y- coordinates.

3. Tell them that mathematicians have agreed to use this order to name points in a coordinate grid. First they read the corresponding number on the x-axis (horizontal line) and then the y-axis (vertical line).

4. Place a new object on the grid and ask participants to name its coordinate numbers.

5. Show how (5,7) is different from (7,5). Demonstrate how if you reverse the x-coordinate and the y-coordinate, you are at a different point. Remember that by convention, x goes first, then y.

6. Have the youth practice locating spots on the grid:
   a. One at a time, have each person select an object and place it on a grid point.
   b. Have another person name the coordinates.
   c. Everyone takes a turn placing an object and others name its coordinates.

Finding Mystery Spots in the Garden

1. Gather the group at the (0,0) point of the clothesline axes. Practice locating points using this large-scale grid. Stand at (0,0) and ask two participants to join you, one to be the "x-axis walker" and another to be the "y-axis walker." Ask the "x-axis walker" to walk to the x-coordinate and stop. Ask the "y-axis walker" to walk to the y-coordinate and stop. As the children walk, the group "counts" off the numbers.

2. Now have the walkers turn and face into the grid. Tell them to walk a straight line into the grid. They will meet at the intersection of the coordinates.

To help youth walk in a straight line, suggest they look at something in front of them beyond the grid as they walk.

3. Give each pair one of the cards with mystery coordinates and ask them to write

MATH IN THE GARDEN

their names on the front. Have them locate the coordinates on their cards by walking the x-axis and y-axis lines into the grid and writing down what they find at each point in the grid.

4. Tell the youth to check back with you about their findings. Help them as needed. Ask questions, such as:
    ❀ How did you locate this place?
    ❀ Which axis did you use first?
    ❀ What would happen if you used the other axis first?

5. As pairs finish finding all of their mystery objects, give them this new challenge. Have them place a stake at a new location in the garden grid for other pairs to locate. Have them record the x- and y-coordinate numbers for their stake on the back of their card and return it to you.

6. Distribute these new mystery coordinates to pairs as they are ready.

Discussing the Activity

Pose a few questions to start a discussion of the activity. Ask:
    ❀ What techniques helped you succeed?
    ❀ If you chose a "treasure" located between two numbers, how did you indicate this coordinate? What are other ways? [used .5 or 1/2, added plus sign to indicate more]
    ❀ How can a coordinate grid be a helpful tool in the garden? [assigning task locations, making a map, recording observations, keeping track of changes over time]
    ❀ How else could a coordinate grid help you? [making a mural, playing a game, building a playhouse, creating a baseball diamond]

More Math in the Garden
(Especially good for ages 10–13)

Negative Numbers Extend the axes beyond the (0,0) to include negative numbers. Make two more numbered lines, one for negative x and one for negative y. Use corresponding colors of tape as you previously used for the positive x- and positive y-axes. Be sure to label these numbers with a negative sign. Find "mystery spots" using the four-quadrant grid.
a. Draw a four-quadrant grid on the databoard, and illustrate locations in each quadrant.
b. Practice finding spots on the databoard grid with the group.
c. Next, go to the garden grid and have the group locate given coordinates.
d. Finally, have pairs determine and record their own "mystery spot" coordinates, and try to find each other's spots.

Comparing the Area of Leaves

Ages 5-8

This activity explores area using number sense and estimation with nonstandard measuring tools.

Children measure the area of a leaf with nonstandard units, such as beans, buttons, and bottle caps. Once they determine the surface area of various leaves, they compare those areas.

What You Need

For Each Pair
- leaf
- clipboard
- overhead transparency
- piece of white paper
- transparency pen
- cup of small flat objects
- journals
- pencils

For the Group
- container of small flat objects of the same kind and size, such as lima beans
- databoard
  – "Measuring Area" steps
- several colors of marking pens

Getting Ready

1. Select a plant with a leaf whose area is smaller than a standard sheet of paper. Depending upon the ages and abilities of the children, select a leaf that will hold a countable number of objects within its area. Five-year-olds are successful with a small leaf like spinach.

2. Identify a flat surface, such as a picnic table or level area of ground, where you can gather the group to set out their clipboards to compare areas.

3. Get about 1 cup of small flat objects of the same kind and approximate size for each pair of children. Dried lima beans work well.

4. Write the "Measuring Area" steps on the databoard.

Here We Go

1. As you walk through the garden, have children look at the sizes and shapes of a variety of leaves. Ask them to show with their hands the size of the largest leaf, then the size of the smallest leaf they found.

2. Tell the children they are going to study different sizes of leaves. Go to your preselected plant to model what the children will do. Demonstrate how to trace a leaf on an overhead transparency.
   a. Carefully place the leaf between the transparency and a clipboard.
   b. Gently trace around the leaf with a transparency pen. This allows the leaf to remain on the plant and lets you keep the outline.

3. Hold the transparency up for all to see. Point to the space inside the leaf tracing. Ask children if they know the mathematical name for the space inside. Tell them it's called the area.

4. Hold up a lima bean and ask how many beans they think it will take to fill the area. Place one inside the area of the leaf and ask them again to estimate how many beans are needed to cover the area. (The single bean provides a benchmark from which to estimate the total needed to fill the area.)

5. Have the children talk about their estimates, share them, and explain their thinking.

6. Place beans, one by one, inside the area of the leaf until you have 10 beans inside the leaf. Let the children revise their estimates.

7. Continue filling the area within the leaf until it is completely covered with one flat layer of beans. Before counting the beans, give the children a final opportunity to revise their estimates.

8. Count out the beans in sets of 10. If there are extra "ones" left, keep them as single beans and count by ones. How many beans did it take? Ask the children if their estimates got closer to the actual number as they had more information about the number of beans to make an estimate.

Measuring the Area of Leaves

1. Go over the "Measuring Area" steps on the databoard. Put the children into pairs and distribute the measuring materials and clipboards.

2. Have the pairs select and trace their leaves. If children are finding it difficult to trace a leaf growing on the plant, help them find a fallen leaf to trace. Guide the pairs through the "Measuring Area" steps and assist as necessary.

3. Regather and have one pair show the outline of their leaf. Let the other children in the group make estimates about how many beans were needed to fill that leaf's area. Have the pair who measured it tell the actual area in beans.

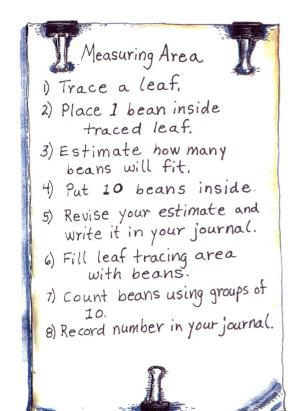

Measuring Area
1) Trace a leaf.
2) Place 1 bean inside traced leaf.
3) Estimate how many beans will fit.
4) Put 10 beans inside.
5) Revise your estimate and write it in your journal.
6) Fill leaf tracing area with beans.
7) Count beans using groups of 10.
8) Record number in your journal.

4. Now record that number inside the leaf outline and place it in the center of the group.

5. Continue with another pair. Have them show their leaf in comparison to the leaf that was just shown. Is it larger, smaller, or about the same size? You can place the transparencies on top of one another to help estimate area.

6. Have children estimate the number of beans needed to cover the second leaf's area. Have the pair share the actual number of beans they counted and record the number in the center of their leaf tracing.

7. Continue until all pairs have shared. After each area is reported, add that leaf to the lineup of the leaves in order of smallest area to largest area.

8. Ask questions such as:
   ❋ What helped you make your estimate?
   ❋ How many leaves have about the same area?
   ❋ What do you notice about the size and shape of the leaves?
   ❋ How do you think leaves help the plant grow?

More Math in the Garden

Comparing Areas Use transparencies with a centimeter grid to compare the areas of leaves using standard units, and then compare the results of both standard and nonstandard measurements.

Manipulating Areas Use string to measure the perimeters of the leaves. Modify the shapes encompassed by the string to see how the areas are affected.

Area & Perimeter of Leaves

Ages 8-13

Youth explore the variety of leaves in the garden. They trace the outline of a leaf and determine its area and perimeter from the tracing. They then analyze and compare the two types of measurements.

Perimeter is the distance around a closed shape. It is a linear measurement. Area is the space inside a closed shape. It is a square measurement.

What You Need

For Each Person
- sheet of 1-centimeter-squared graph paper
- 30-centimeter piece of string
- journal
- pencil and crayons

For Each Pair
- clipboard or table workspace
- centimeter ruler
- scissors

For the Group
- databoard
- marking pens
- 1-centimeter-squared graph paper
- meter stick

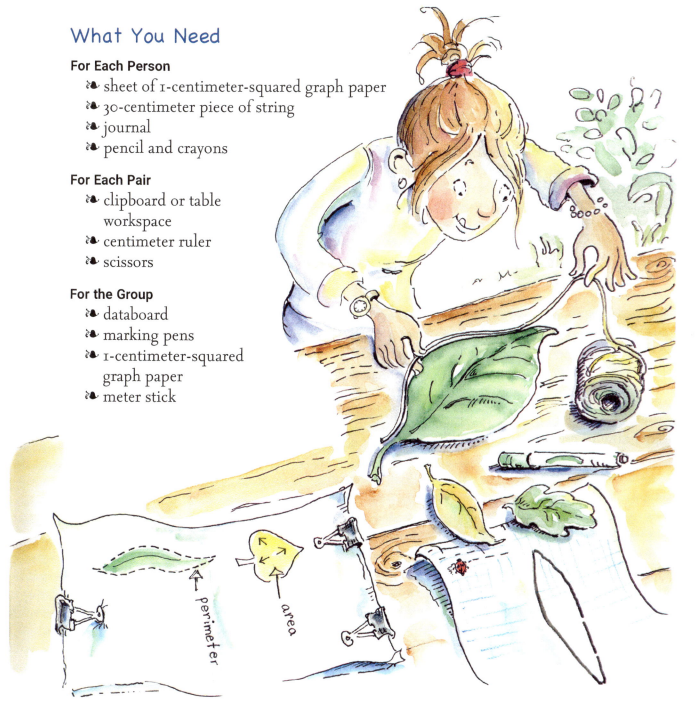

MATH IN THE GARDEN

Getting Ready

1. Make sure there are leaves you can pick in the garden, otherwise bring a few stems with leaves that vary in size and shape. Avoid difficult-to-measure leaves, for example ones that are lobed, jagged, larger than a hand span, or smaller than a thumb.

2. Draw illustrations of leaves on the databoard labeled with area and perimeter near the illustrations.

Here We Go

1. Show the youth how to pick a leaf carefully from the lower and back part of a plant. Have everyone collect and observe a leaf.

2. Ask what the distance around the entire leaf is called. [perimeter]

3. Have them note the different sizes of the various leaves. Ask if they know what all the space within the perimeter is called. [area]

4. Show your illustration of leaves on the databoard with the area and perimeter labeled. With their help, define a perimeter and an area of a leaf.

5. Ask the youth if they have ever used an area or perimeter measurement. You may want to give them an example of buying a rug for a room or a belt for pants.

What's the Area?

1. Ask if anyone knows how area is measured and described. Tell them it is described in square units. Show a sheet of centimeter-squared graph paper. Shade in one square. Tell them this is a unit of square measurement — a square centimeter — and it is how they are going to measure the area of leaves.

2. With the help of a volunteer, trace your leaf onto a sheet of centimeter-squared paper. Show the tracing.

3. Ask the youth what strategies they would use to determine the area. Tell them they need to count all the squares inside the leaf to find the area. The partial squares need to be added up also. They will record the area on the leaf tracing, as so:

Area = ___ square centimeters.

4. Have each youth work with a partner to help each other trace leaves on centimeter-squared graph paper and calculate the area.

5. When everyone has finished, ask volunteers to explain their various strategies for counting the squares, and partial squares, to calculate the area of their leaves.

6. Organize the centimeter paper leaf tracings from the smallest area to the greatest area. Start by asking for the leaf with the smallest area, and then find the leaf with the greatest area. With those two benchmarks, line up the other tracings from smallest to greatest area between the benchmarks.

7. Ask:
    ❀ Were you surprised by the placement of any of the leaves? Why?
    ❀ Do you notice any shape similarities among the leaves with the greatest areas?
    ❀ Do you notice any shape similarities among the leaves with the smallest areas?
    ❀ Are there leaves of dissimilar shape that have similar areas?
    ❀ How might leaf shape be helpful to a plant? [large round ones have more surface area to catch low levels of sunlight such as on a forest floor, long thin leaves can bend in the wind, small leaves can reduce water loss]

What's the Perimeter?

1. Have a volunteer help you demonstrate how to use string to measure the distance around the perimeter of a leaf. Once the string borders the entire leaf, cut the string and retain the measured length.

2. Hold up the string and ask what it represents. When everyone identifies it as the perimeter, point out that perimeter is a linear measurement. It only has length — unlike a square unit of measurement that has both length and width.

3. Use a centimeter ruler or meter stick to measure the cut string. Write this perimeter measurement in centimeters next to the leaf tracing, as so:
Perimeter = _____ centimeters.

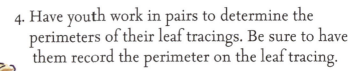

4. Have youth work in pairs to determine the perimeters of their leaf tracings. Be sure to have them record the perimeter on the leaf tracing.

5. Once finished, have the youth compare the perimeter strings with the leaf tracings themselves.

6. Now organize the strings with their leaves from the shortest perimeter to the longest perimeter. Start by asking for the string with the shortest perimeter, and then find the string with the longest perimeter. With those two benchmarks, line up the other leaf tracings and strings.

7. Ask for observations about the perimeters of leaves, using these two displays of the perimeter — the strings and the leaf tracings themselves. Ask:
   ❀ Does the leaf with the longest perimeter contain the most area?

8. With the following demonstration, recap the difference between area and perimeter. Ask a volunteer to tie a loop of string as long as the longest perimeter, and then make a long and very skinny shape. Invite the group to describe the area of this shape. [small, narrow, not much area at all] Now ask the volunteer to make a circle out of the same loop and invite descriptions of this area. [much bigger than the last one] Note the surprise that the same perimeter can have more than one area.

More Math in the Garden

Creating Different Areas Challenge each youth to use a perimeter string to make a shape with the largest possible area, and then with the same string to make a shape with the smallest possible area. What common characteristics do the shapes with the largest (or smallest) area share?

Creating Different Perimeters Challenge youth to use the area measurement of their leaves to create different shapes that have the same area but different perimeters.

Half of a Half of My Garden Plot

Ages 8–13

This activity demonstrates fractional parts of a whole by consecutively dividing an area by increments of one-half. After the divisions are made, the whole can be seen as the sum of all its parts.

Youth design a garden by dividing their own plot into smaller parts. They start by dividing their entire plot in half, and then take half of one of the two halves to create two quarter plots. They continue until the size of the last fractional part of their plot is the area needed to grow a single plant. The youth then plant the plots and can enjoy watching their beautiful patchwork grow.

What You Need

For Each Team of Four
- ball of string
- 24-foot string tied in a loop
- 14 to 20 craft sticks
- 1 bright crayon — red, blue, or purple
- scissors
- ruler
- journals
- pencils

For the Group
- lawn area
- garden plot, 4' x 8'
- extra craft sticks
- seedlings to plant
- several yardsticks

Getting Ready

1. Cut a 24-foot length of string for each group and tie the ends to form a loop. These will be used to outline practice plots and your garden plot.

2. On a lawn near your garden, stake out a 4' x 8' plot for your demonstration using craft sticks. If you have time constraints for the activity, stake out a plot for each team as well.

Here We Go

1. Gather the group around your demonstration plot.

2. Inform them that when growing plants it is important to know the amount of space each plant needs as a mature plant.

3. Hold up a plant, such as a tomato, and tell them that the area needed for a full-grown plant is 1 square foot. Today we are going to learn a method to divide garden beds so our plants will have enough room.

4. Tell the youth you are going to divide this plot into two equal halves. You then will divide one of the halves in half again. You will do this until you have a plot that is just the right size for growing one plant.

5. Have volunteers help you section off the demonstration plot. Have one person tie the end of the string to a craft stick and stick it in the ground in one corner of the plot. Ask another individual to unwind the ball of string along the length of the plot to the opposite end.

Scissors make a handy tool for "punching" a hole into the soil for the craft stick.

6. Cut the string so it measures the length of the plot with a little extra to spare. Let the youth remain there, holding the point on the string that reached the end of the plot.

Finding the Midpoint

1. Ask the group how to determine the point on the string that is half the distance from one end of the plot to the other end. Let them estimate the location of the midpoint. Have another volunteer pinch the point on the string that they think is the midpoint.

2. Show how to "fold" the string into two equal lengths by having the individual with the loose end of the string (untied end) walk back to the end that is tied to the craft stick.

3. Look at the point where the volunteer is pinching the string and the two lengths of strings that are created by the fold. Does the folded string match up so that each of the two new lengths are equal? If not, adjust the lengths of string so they are equal and have the volunteer pinching the string move to

the midpoint. Once the midpoint is established, ask the volunteer put a craft stick in the ground to mark the point.

4. Have the youth with the untied end of the string walk back along the side of the plot, tie the string to a craft stick, and put the stick in the ground.

5. Cut another piece of string that can span the width of the plot with a little extra to spare. Tie one end of the string to the craft stick marking the midpoint, and let someone take the other end to the opposite side of the plot. Ask for ideas of how to make 90° angles at the divisions.

Half of a Half of a Half of a …

1. Have the group look at the plot — now divided into two equal areas. Tell them you want to divide one of the halves in half. Ask for ideas of how to proceed.

2. Guide the group in finding the midpoint along the string that was just laid. Use a piece of string to divide the half into two equal areas as you did above. Point out that these two new "halves" together are equal to the first half. They are "half" of the original half. Each is one-fourth of the whole plot. Look at the three areas that you have created and name the fractional parts of the plot. [one-half, one-fourth, and one-fourth]

3. Choose one of the one-fourth areas to divide again. Divide this piece into two halves. Point out that each of these "halves" is one-eighth of the whole plot, and that as more halves are made, parts are quickly getting smaller in area.

4. Continue taking halves until you have a 1-foot-square plot. Tell them that this is the space needed for one full-grown plant and so you will stop dividing at this point.

5. Have the youth tell you how the plot was subdivided into parts by successively taking "half of a half." Check that they know why you stopped where you did. [The plant needs a 1-foot-square plot.]

Dividing the Plots

1. Once everyone grasps how to divide a garden plot, assign each team to their own 4' x 8' plot on the lawn and tell them to stake out their plot with the string loop and craft sticks. They will then subdivide their plot by halves until they create a 1-foot-square area for a plant.

2. When all teams are finished, have the group look at one of the team plots.
   Ask guiding questions, such as:
   ❀ Does it look like the demonstration plot? How does it differ?
   ❀ How many times did you divide the plot in half?

3. Visit the remaining plots looking for similarities and differences. Assist youth to identify the fractional parts of their plots.

4. To help them identify the four one-fourths that make up the whole garden plot, have two youths stretch another string across the undivided half of the plot. It is important to define this fractional part in terms of the whole plot.

5. If you feel that your group needs more practice with fractional parts of the whole, do the same with the one-eighth area.

Planting in the Garden

1. Gather your group around the planting bed in the garden. Together divide the plot using the same "half of a half of a half" technique until you produce one-foot-square plots.

2. Show the youths the seedlings you brought to plant. Inform them of the size of the area needed by each when it is a mature plant. Have them look at the seedlings and decide where each plant should go. They may need to divide some of the areas into smaller plots.

3. Have youth label craft sticks with the names of their plants. Place the appropriate labeled sticks next to seedlings. Water the seedlings.

More Math in the Garden

Dividing Again Challenge the youth to divide a plot using the same "half of a half of a half" technique, but in such a way that the fractional parts have different shapes. Be sure they can prove that the smallest fractional parts have an equal area.

Ratios of Shoots and Roots

Ages 8-13

This activity uses number sense, estimation, and comparison to determine ratios.

Youth harvest crops then measure and compare the lengths of the stem and roots of plants such as radishes, carrots, green onions, and lettuce to determine the ratios of shoots to roots. This activity is great to do with any plants when you need to weed the garden.

What You Need

For Each Pair
- trowel
- metric ruler
- cardboard
- journals
- pencils

For the Group
- 2 databoards
  – sample plant drawing
  – "Shoot/Root Table"
- 3 colors of marking pens

MATH IN THE GARDEN

Getting Ready

1. Collect cardboard that will support the length of a harvested plant while it is being measured.

2. Mark the area of the garden where the youth will harvest crops, and identify plants that need to be protected. Dig up a sample plant.

3. Draw a horizontal line across the middle of a databoard to represent the surface of the soil. Sketch the root of a plant below ground and the shoot above ground.

4. On the second databoard, draw a table to record shoot and root measurements and ratios.

Here We Go

1. Hold up the drawing of the plant and ask:
   ❀ How do roots help a plant? [take in water, nutrients, and minerals; anchor the plant in the ground; store food for the plant]
   ❀ How have farmers taken advantage of the natural ability of plants to make and store food? [growing crops such as sweet potatoes, carrots, radishes]
   ❀ How does the length of this shoot (the stem and leaves above ground) compare with the length of the root? Is it longer, shorter, or about the same?

2. Explain that they will dig up edible plants and compare the estimated lengths of the roots and shoots. Encourage them to predict if the plants will have roots that are longer than, equal to, or shorter than, their shoots.

3. Demonstrate how to carefully dig up and measure a plant such as a radish. Gently shake the soil off the roots. Arrange the plant along the soil line drawn on the databoard and next to the sketch of the plant. Extend, but don't stretch, the green shoot above and the roots below the soil line.

4. Ask a volunteer to help you mark the top of the shoot and the end of the longest root on the databoard. Use a metric ruler to measure the roots and shoot to the nearest centimeter, and record the results on the "Shoot/Root Table." Write "cm" after the measurements to note the metric unit.

5. Demonstrate how to round measurements up or down to the nearest centimeter. The goal is to use whole numbers for the ratios. For example, if the length of the shoot is more than 8 cm and less than 8 1/2 cm, then we round down to 8 cm.

6. Have a volunteer assist you to add the rounded numbers for the root and shoot lengths to get a whole number for the estimated total length. Record that number on the databoard.

In some cases the process of rounding up and down to the nearest whole number will result in the estimated total length being one integer higher or lower than the actual measured length of the plant. This small difference should not matter because we are looking at the overall relationship between the shoot size and root size and not at a precise measurement of total length.

Measuring Shoots and Roots

1. Divide the youth into pairs and direct them to dig up a plant and draw it in their journals.

2. Tell them to arrange their plants on the cardboard and draw a line to represent the soil surface. They then measure the shoots and roots, and record their results in their journals and on the "Shoot/Root Table."

3. Circulate among the pairs, assisting where needed.

Finding the Ratio

1. Gather the group to discuss their measurements posted on the "Shoot/Root Table." Ask:
   ❦ Who has a plant with a shoot that is longer than the root?
   ❦ Who has a plant with a shoot that is shorter than the root?
   ❦ Were there any plants with shoots and roots about equal?

2. Explain that they will use ratios to compare the shoots to the roots. A ratio can be shown as two items separated by a colon. As an example, write "S:R" on the table (see illustration, page 46), and below it enter the ratio for the first set of plant measurements. As you move down the table, have youth identify the ratio for each pair of shoot and root measurements.

A ratio is a comparison of two amounts using division. It can be shown several ways, 8:12, 8/12, or 8 to 12.

MATH IN THE GARDEN

Shoot/Root Table

Plant Name	Shoot Length	Root Length	Total Length	Ratio S:R	Shoot to Root S/R
Radish	8 cm	12 cm	20 cm	8:12	8/12
Carrot	11 cm	22 cm	33 cm	11:22	11/22

3. Have volunteers help you arrange the plants into one of three categories, shoots greater than roots, shoots and roots about the same, and shoots less than roots. Use different colors of marking pens to color code the list of plants. Ask:
    - ❀ What are similarities within each group?
    - ❀ Do you notice any trends?
    - ❀ How might ratios help us to compare the harvested plants?

4. Tell the group that botanists have noticed that very young plants often have large differences between the size of their shoots and roots. As plants mature, the size differences between shoots and roots often become less. Unhealthy plants may show great differences between the size and quantity of shoots versus roots. There are many exceptions to these trends. Ask:
    - ❀ How might looking at shoot/root ratios be useful to gardeners? [estimating the size of the root crop by only looking at its leaves]

5. Ask youth to record their ideas in their journals and complete their ratio records for their plants.

More Math in the Garden

Finding Percentages Introduce percents as another way to analyze the size relationship between roots and shoots. To determine the percent of the plant that is shoot, divide the shoot length by the total plant length and multiply that number by 100.

Shoot/Root Weights Have students use scales to compare the weights of roots and shoots. See "Weighing the Garden Harvest," page 79.

Weed Adaptations Plants that are adapted for harsh environments often exhibit interesting shoot/root ratios. Have youth investigate hardy weeds that survive on the compacted paths and edges of the garden.

Soil + Water Profile

Ages 8-13

This activity explores measuring fractions in an inch and determining fractional equivalents.

Youth measure the layers revealed by mixing soil and water, then calculate the proportion of organic and inorganic components. This activity is best done following "What's in Garden Soil?" (page 139), an exploration of the organic and inorganic components of soil.

What You Need

For Each Pair
- clear, 3-inch seasoning bottle or vial (containers for all pairs must be the same size)
- ruler (1/8-inch calibration)
- plastic spoon
- fine-tip permanent pen
- journals
- pencils and crayons

For the Group
- 2 databoards
  – "Soil + Water Profile" chart
  – "Soil Test Steps"
- 3 colors of marking pens
- table salt
- source of water
- labeled commercial garden soil mix that does not contain Perlite™ or vermiculite

Getting Ready

1. Draw the "Soil + Water Profile" demonstration chart.

2. List the "Soil Test Steps" on the second databoard.

3. Assemble the equipment.

4. Check that your commercial garden mix does not contain inorganic substances like vermiculite, which will float along with the organic materials that youth will be measuring.

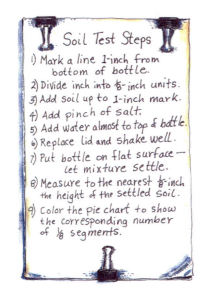

Soil Test Steps
1) Mark a line 1-inch from bottom of bottle.
2) Divide inch into 1/8-inch units.
3) Add soil up to 1-inch mark.
4) Add pinch of salt.
5) Add water almost to top of bottle.
6) Replace lid and shake well.
7) Put bottle on flat surface — let mixture settle.
8) Measure to the nearest 1/8-inch the height of the settled soil.
9) Color the pie chart to show the corresponding number of 1/8 segments.

MATH IN THE GARDEN

Here We Go

1. Distribute rulers. Guide a quick review of how to measure in inches.
   - How many small equal measures is the inch divided into? [8]
   - What do you call one fractional part of the inch? [one eighth, 1/8]
   - Find the line that shows the halfway point of the inch; what is it called? [one half, 1/2]
   - How many eighth lengths equal one half? [four, 4/8]
   - How many eighths are in 1/4? [two, 2/8]; in 2/4? [four, 4/8]; in 3/4? [six, 6/8]
   - When using a ruler, where do you begin measuring something? [at the "0" point; note that this may not be the end of the ruler]

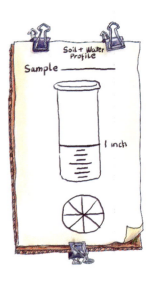

2. Have youth look at the pie chart below the "Soil + Water Profile" and identify the eight equal parts. Remind them that each fractional part is called an eighth.
   - How many eighths would they need to color to cover half of the area of the circle? [four, 4/8]
   - How is the pie chart similar to the inch diagram? [Both are divided into 8 equal parts.]

Demonstrating a Soil + Water Profile

1. Share with the group that gardeners need to know the composition of their soil so that they can make amendments for the best plant growth. Introduce the "Soil + Water Profile" test as a great method to determine what's in a mixture of soil and the relative amount of each component. Use the commercial garden mix to demonstrate the following:
   a. Use a ruler and permanent pen to mark a line 1 inch from the bottom of a small clear bottle. Subdivide the inch into 1/8 measures.
   b. Fill the bottle to the 1-inch mark with the soil to be tested, and add a big pinch of salt.
   c. Add water almost to the top of the bottle, cover, and shake vigorously.
   d. Place the bottle on a flat surface, and let the material settle for several minutes. Be careful not to disturb the bottle.

The added salt speeds up the settling process, allowing the water to clear faster than it would with tap water.

2. While waiting for soil to settle, ask youth to copy the "Soil + Water Profile" drawing and pie chart in their journals.

3. Once the water in the bottle has cleared, ask: "What do you think settled to the bottom?" [rocks, sand, silt, clay, heavy things] "Are these organic or inorganic?" [Inorganic materials usually sink to the bottom.]

4. Ask a volunteer to help you check carefully (without moving the bottle) the thickness of the inorganic layer at the bottom. Point out that the layer on the bottom varies slightly from place to place. Help them agree on the method that everyone will use in measuring the inorganic layer on the bottom.

5. Record the amount in eighths on the drawing of the "Soil + Water Profile," and have the youth record the commercial mix results in their journals.

What is Floating on Top?

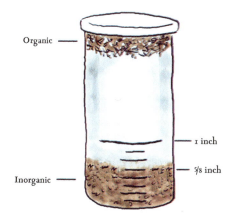

1. Ask the youth what they think is floating on top. Have them refer to the ingredients on commercial mix label for ideas. (Most commercial mixes contain bark, which is organic and floats.)

2. Invite volunteers to tell you the size of the organic layer without actually measuring the floating materials. Wait at least 20 seconds for a reply before guiding the group through the following steps:
   a. How much of the bottle did you fill with soil? [1 inch, 8/8]
   b. How much inorganic material is left at the bottom? [for this example, it is 5/8 inch]
   c. With only this information, how can we determine the amount of floating organic material? [Subtract the amount of inorganic from the amount of soil you started with. For this example, 8/8 – 5/8 = ?/8]
   d. How much organic material is floating at the top? [in this example, 3/8 inch]

3. Ask for assistance in coloring and labeling the pie chart to represent the fractional organic and inorganic parts of the soil. Check that the youth make the connection between the 1/8-inch measures on the sample and the 1/8 segments on the pie chart.

Measuring Garden Soil Profiles

1. Explain that each pair will conduct a water test on a sample of soil they collect from the garden. Review the "Soil Test Steps" listed on the databoard, distribute the equipment, and let pairs collect their soil samples.

2. Remind the pairs to label their bottle with "1 inch" and subdivide it into 1/8-inch measures before adding the soil.

3. As you circulate among the pairs, check their measuring methods. Encourage them to measure the profile of the soil sample carefully, then record

Explain that most soil organisms are desirable and harmless. If small invertebrates are discovered floating in the water profile, they will probably survive the dunking if the pairs pour the sample back into the garden after quickly taking the measurements. The tiny amount of salt in the water will not harm the plants or animals.

their measurement on their journal drawings. Be sure they can determine the organic part of the soil sample using the data from the inorganic measurement. Assist them in coloring in the pie chart that shows the fractional parts of inorganic and organic soil.

Analyzing the Results

1. Gather the group to discuss their findings. Ask a pair that has recorded its measurements and colored the pie chart in a clear and accurate way to share their findings with the group.

2. Ask several questions to stimulate their thinking about the similarities and differences between the commercial mix and the garden soil:
   * Which soil has the most inorganic material?
   * In that sample, how many 1/8 inches are inorganic?
   * How many 1/8 segments of the circle graph represent the inorganic part of the soil sample?
   * Which soil has the most organic material? How many 1/8 inches?
   * How many 1/8 segments of the circle graph represent the fractional part of the soil sample that is organic?

3. Have other pairs share the results of their "Soil + Water Profiles." Ask:
   * Who has the garden soil sample with the most organic material? The least?
   * Why do you think you found more organic material in your sample? [sampled a different location, estimated the layers differently, took the measurement right away before some of the organic material sank to the bottom]
   * Why is organic material important to gardens? [keeps soil loose, provides air pockets and nutrients for soil fertility, retains moisture]
   * What does inorganic material contribute to a garden? [provides soil structure and minerals]

4. Remind the youth that a goal of the "Soil + Water Profile" test is to gather information to help improve the soil in the garden. Suggest that in future sessions they can help improve the soil through composting, mulching, and removing rocks. Then they can re-test the soil and compare the new results to the results from this sampling.

More Math in the Garden

Improving the Soil Have children create an area of "improved" soil and compare the growth of seeds planted in the experimental area with seeds planted in the standard garden soil.

Determining Organic Percentages By converting their fractions, have youth estimate the percentage of inorganic and organic parts of the soil, for example 2/8 is 25%.

CHAPTER TWO
Measurement

Measurement permeates our everyday lives. Each day is measured in hours, minutes, and seconds. We use units of measure to determine length, weight, mass, area, volume, and temperature of common objects. A seed packet has information related to the plant's growth, such as number of days to germinate, depth to plant the seeds, spacing between seedlings, and height of full-grown plant. Measurement systems provide a universal language for quantifying and communicating amounts.

Measurement often begins with comparisons — which item is heavier? Smaller? Cooler? A person must select the most appropriate unit and tool for measurement and decide the level of accuracy required by a particular task. In some cases, nonuniform, nonstandard units of measure, such as hand spans, are convenient to use in estimating distances. The length of the hand span can then be converted to standard units such as inches and centimeters.

Measurement is closely connected to geometry. Perimeter, area, volume, and angles are all dependent upon units of measurement. In some cases, measurement and geometry connect to algebra — such as the formulas to determine area and volume of geometric shapes. Measurement also connects to statistics through comparative data analysis.

The activities in this section provide opportunities to use the metric and English systems of measurement, as well as nonstandard units of measure. Children will plan plots, measure the harvest, check soil composition, and investigate growth over time. Through these activities, they explore the length, area, volume, and weight of items in the garden.

Hand Spans

Ages 5-13

Gardeners often use hand spans, paces, and other nonstandard measures to plant. In this activity, children use their hands and rulers to estimate and measure the length of objects in the garden.

This activity explores length using a hand span, a nonstandard and nonuniform unit of measurement. A ruler is a tool with a standard unit of measurement, such as an inch or centimeter, inscribed on it.

What You Need

For Each Pair
- ruler (inches or centimeters)
- journals
- pencils

For the Group
- databoard
- colored marking pens

Getting Ready

1. Walk through the garden and plan what objects and plants the children will measure using their hand spans.

2. Gather rulers that have a zero labeled at the starting point.

3. For younger children use rulers that show inches; for older children use a centimeter ruler. If your rulers show both measurement systems, tape over the side you don't want the children to use.

MATH IN THE GARDEN

Here We Go

1. Tell the children they will learn methods that farmers have used for thousands of years to measure objects in the garden. Ask:
   ❊ What do you use to measure the length of an object?
   ❊ What kinds of things might you measure in the garden?

2. Using your hand, demonstrate the length of a hand span:
   a. Spread your hand on the surface of the databoard, and mark the outer tips of your thumb and pinky finger.
   b. Using a ruler, connect the two points with a straight line and label the length "My Hand Span."

3. Have children demonstrate their hand spans with a partner by holding up their hands (with fingers spread apart), palm to palm, fingers lined up. Do any children have the same hand span? (Some may; however, many will differ slightly in length.)

4. Model how to measure an object using your hand span. Ask a volunteer to measure a second object that is longer than one hand span. Remind the individual to have a fully extended hand span while measuring. As a group, determine how to count partial spans, such as "about half" a span or "a bit more" than a span.

Hand Span Hunt

1. Have the children go into the garden on a "Hand Span Hunt" to find three things that are approximately the same length as their hand spans.

2. Regather the group and have the children share what they measured. Ask them how their hand span measurements could help them in the garden.

3. If no one mentions it, point out that gardeners often use their hand spans as a quick way to estimate lengths of things in the garden, such as how much room to leave between plants, stepping stones, and garden beds.

Measuring a Hand Span

1. Tell the children they will measure the length of their own hand span with a ruler. Knowing their own hand span length will allow them to compare hand span measurements among their group.

2. Ask if anyone has used a ruler to measure things, and if they used inches or centimeters.

3. Distribute the rulers and ask the pairs to identify the "0" starting point. Depending on the age of your group, ask them to find the 1-inch mark (or 1-centimeter mark), the 6-inch mark (15-centimeter mark), and 12-inch mark (30-centimeter mark).

4. Have the children, with a partner's help, trace their hand spans in their journals, measure their hand spans with the ruler, and record the results.

5. Ask children to report the lengths of their hand spans and compare hand span measurements among the group.

Hand spans vary, so if you know the length of your own hand you can make fairly accurate estimates when measuring.

Estimating and Measuring in the Garden

1. Have the pairs go on another hunt to measure three things using their hand spans. Ask them to draw the items in their journals and record the number of hand span lengths. For example: leaf = half a hand span, brick = 1 hand span.

2. Gather the group and have the pairs share what they measured. Show them how to determine the number of inches (or centimeters) for each item by converting their hand spans to the standard units.

3. To give children practice using their new hand span "measuring tool," hold up an item from the garden, and ask them to estimate its length. Ask them to record their estimates in their journals in hand spans and in inches or centimeters.

4. As a group, measure the item with a ruler. Have the children record the actual measurement in their journals, and compare their estimates with the actual measurement.

5. Give additional objects to the pairs to measure with the rulers. Have them record their measurements in their journals. Encourage children to share and discuss their estimates and measurements.

6. Ask the group why knowing how to measure with your hand span is a useful skill. What are some things at home you could measure with your hand span? [dinner plate, television screen, pet, height of a stair]

The Hand Span Song

Lyrics by youth Kelsey Connolly

Children enjoy displaying their hand spans in time with this song that follows the tune of "If you're happy and you know it, clap your hands."

Refrain
If you want to measure something, use your hand span!
If you want to measure something, use your hand span!
Thumb and pinkie open wide.
It's an excellent measuring guide.
If you want to measure something, use your hand span!

If you want to plant some seeds in row, Go!
If you want to plant some seeds in row, Go!
Thumb and pinkie open wide,
with no ruler at your side.
You can use your hand span nicely in a row, Go!

Refrain
Do you see your green beans growing big and tall? Yea!
Do you see your green beans growing big and tall? Yea!
Use your handy measuring guide.
Thumb and pinkie open wide.
If you want to measure green beans, use your hands, Yea!

Refrain

More Math in the Garden

Brown Bag Secret Hide a long vegetable like a zucchini in a brown bag. Tell children that the mystery vegetable is safe to touch. Pass the bag around so that everyone has a chance to reach in and feel the object. When they touch it, they are not to say what it is, rather they are to silently estimate how long it is in inches. After everyone has had a chance to estimate its length, ask what they think is in the bag. Reveal the object and ask a pair of children to measure it. How close were they in their estimates?

Hand Span Planting Have the children use their hand spans to measure the length of a planting bed. Use hand spans to space the seedlings in the bed.

Centimeter by Centimeter

Ages 5-8

This activity introduces the metric units centimeter and meter.

Children sharpen their observation skills as they measure the heights of their small plants using centimeter rulers. They draw their plants, record the measurements, and share the measurements with the group.

What You Need

For Each Pair
- 30-cm ruler
- journals
- pencils and crayons

For the Group
- 30-cm ruler
- 12-in ruler
- meter stick (100 cm)
- databoard
- colored marking pens

Getting Ready

1. Select an area of the garden with many plants that are less than 30 centimeters high for the children to measure and record the heights. Pick one plant to use for a measurement demonstration.

2. Gather metric rulers that have a zero labeled at the starting point. If your rulers show both centimeters and inches, tape over the side with inches so children aren't confused by the two measurement systems.

MATH IN THE GARDEN

Here We Go

1. Gather the children and ask questions about measurement, such as:
   ❋ Have you measured before? If so, what?
   ❋ What did you use to measure the object?
       It is likely that at least one child will be familiar with a ruler.

2. If a child mentions a ruler as a tool, ask what units of measurement were on the ruler. Usually, children know inches. Ask them to show a measurement of 1 inch using their fingers. Show the inch ruler to help them adjust the distance between their two fingers to equal about an inch.

3. Ask about centimeters.
   ❋ Has anyone ever heard of a centimeter?
   ❋ Is it longer or shorter than an inch?

4. Show them a centimeter ruler to help them adjust the distance between two fingers to equal about a centimeter. Allow children to compare the two measurement units. Explain that they will use the metric unit, centimeter, to measure plants in the garden.

Working with Centimeters

1. Divide your group into pairs and distribute the 30-cm rulers. Check that children can identify 1 centimeter. Ask how many centimeters are on the ruler. [30]

2. Send the pairs into the garden to find something that is about 30-cm long.

3. Regroup and ask them what they found that is about 30-cm long.

4. Ask how they could measure something longer than 30 centimeters. Show a meter stick and tell them its name. Ask them to predict how many 30-cm rulers are needed to equal the length of the meter stick. Have them tell their prediction to their partner.

MATH IN THE GARDEN

5. Lay the meter stick on the ground where everyone can see it. Have one child place a 30-cm ruler at the end of the meter stick where the numbering starts.

6. Have the children estimate how many 30-cm rulers are needed. Have another child place another ruler at the 30-cm mark of the first ruler. Finally, have a third child add one more 30-cm ruler. Ask:
   ❃ Does the length of the meter stick equal three 30-cm rulers? [No, it is 10 cm longer.]
   ❃ If they added another 30-cm ruler, would it be equal? Why or why not? [Four 30-cm rulers would be too long.]

7. Add a fourth 30-cm ruler. They will see that four 30-cm rulers are longer than the meter stick. Show the point where the distance of the 30-cm rulers equals a meter. It will be three 30-cm rulers and 10 cm of the fourth ruler. Establish that 1 meter contains 100 centimeters.

Measuring Plant Heights

1. As a group, go to the less-than-30-cm-plant you selected.

2. Demonstrate on the databoard how you want the children to proceed. Begin by writing the name of the plant and the date, and then draw a simple picture of the plant including the soil line.

3. Place your ruler at the base of the plant. Point out that the end you place closest to the soil has the number zero on it. Measure the height of the plant from its base to its top.

4. Ask a volunteer to help you "read" the height of the plant. Hold up the ruler with your finger marking the height measurement of the plant. Have the child read the height in centimeters while you record the height of the plant on the databoard.

5. Explain that each partner will select a different plant to draw, measure, and record the height in his or her journal. Partners will compare the measurements of their two plants.

Comparing Plant Heights

1. Once the children finish measuring, call the group together. Have the partners compare the two plants they measured. Ask:
   - Which was taller?
   - How many more centimeters tall?

2. If you have a large group, have the pairs select their tallest plant to compare and rank the heights. Help children line up with their drawings in the following groups:
   a. Compare plants 10 cm or less tall. Rank from shortest to tallest.
   b. Compare plants 11 cm to 20 cm tall. Rank from shortest to tallest.
   c. Compare plants 21 cm to 30 cm tall. Rank from shortest to tallest.

3. Have the remaining partners rank their shorter plants in the same manner, facing the other row of children.

4. Ask questions about the groupings of plants by height, such as:
   - Which height range had the most plants in it? (0–10, 11-20, 21-30)
   - How many plants shared the same height?
   - Which type of plant measured was shortest?
   - Which type of plant measured was tallest?

5. Ask the children to predict which plants they think will grow the most in height in a week. Suggest that they check on their plants at a future date to see how many centimeters the plants have grown.

More Math in the Garden

Revisiting & Measuring Plants Have the children monitor the growth of their plants in one-week intervals. What do they notice about the growth? Partners can compare the growth of their two plants.

Ideal Growing Time During your ideal growing season, start seedlings you know grow at a dramatic rate. Chart the growth of these plants over time.

Inch by Inch Read the book *Inch by Inch* by Leo Lionni about measurement in the garden. In this story an inchworm measures various items before inching away from being eaten. Children can use an inch measurement tool to measure an item in the garden. They can also compare inches to centimeters.

Garden Harvest – Measuring Length

Ages 5-13

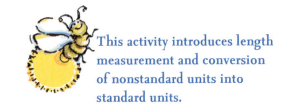

This activity introduces length measurement and conversion of nonstandard units into standard units.

Youth harvest fruits and vegetables from the garden and use string and rulers to find the length and circumference of each item picked. They compare their measurements and discuss how the practice of measuring produce is helpful to farmers.

What You Need

For Each Pair
- string or ribbon, 18 inches
- ruler (inches or centimeters)
- journals
- pencils and crayons

For the Group
- databoard
  - fruit drawing
  - "Measurements" chart
- colored marking pens
- yardstick or meter stick
- harvest items (beans, squash, cucumbers, carrots)

Getting Ready

1. Walk through the garden and plan what the children will harvest and measure. Pick a fruit that is long and somewhat irregular for your demonstration, and sketch it on the databoard.

2. Gather rulers that have a zero labeled at the starting point. For younger children, use rulers that show inches; for older children, use a centimeter ruler. If your rulers show both measurement systems and this is the first measuring activity, tape over the side you don't want children to use.

MATH IN THE GARDEN

3. Get nonstretch string or ribbon that does not fray at the ends, and cut lengths of about 18 inches for partners to use as flexible measurers.

Here We Go

1. Gather the children and tell them that they will help harvest and measure fruits such as cucumbers that have been growing in the garden. Explain that botanists call the part of a plant that holds and protects seeds the fruit. Ask:
   ❧ What fruits are growing in our garden? [beans, tomatoes, zucchini, lemons]
   ❧ What else besides fruits might we harvest? [broccoli, lettuce, radishes]
   ❧ Why do you think it is important to measure the harvest? [to know how well your crops are doing, find out how much food there is to eat or sell]

2. Show them your irregular fruit, such as a curvy cucumber, and ask for their ideas about how to measure it.
   ❧ What kinds of measurements might we make? [length, width, circumference, weight, volume]
   ❧ What tools could we use to measure the length? [ruler, hand span, measuring tape, string]

3. Have children show you, using their fingers, the length of an inch (or centimeter). Distribute rulers to the pairs and have them check the measurement. Direct their attention to the zero point. If they haven't used rulers before, give them time to become familiar with this tool.

4. Hold up your databoard with the drawing of the fruit you will use for the demonstration, and pass the fruit around for the children to observe. Ask:
   - ❦ What advantages do you see for using this string as a measurer? [can follow the surface of the fruit; is longer than one ruler-length]
   - ❦ At what point on the fruit could we start the length measurement? [stem end, other end]

5. Explain that everyone will use the same method of starting the string at the place where the stem was attached and extending the string to the growing tip of the fruit. If a stem is still attached to the fruit, point out that it should not be included in the measurement. Ask:
   - ❦ Why is it important that we all use the same measuring method? [so we can compare our data]

6. Model how a pair will work together as partners using the string to measure the length of a fruit or vegetable. Invite a volunteer to be your partner:
   a. Have your partner hold one end of the string at the stem end of the fruit and extend the remainder of the string along the length of the fruit, smoothing it but not stretching it.
   b. Pinch the end of the string at the point that measures the length of the fruit.
   c. Lay the string along a ruler, beginning at the zero point.
   d. Ask your partner to read the measurement, and label the length and units on the drawing. Show them how to round their measurements to the nearest half-inch or half-centimeter.

MATH IN THE GARDEN

e. Demonstrate how to measure the circumference of the fruit at the approximate midpoint of its length, and label that measurement, noting the units.

Measuring the Harvest

1. Review the steps for harvesting, drawing, measuring, and recording the data, and distribute the journals and materials. Let the harvest begin!

2. Circulate among the pairs, encouraging them to draw and label the details of their fruit. Check to make certain that they are measuring the string from the "0" point on the ruler.

3. As pairs complete their records of length and circumference in their journals, have them record the results on the group "Measurements" chart.

4. Gather the group to discuss their findings. Ask questions to guide the children to make true statements about their measurements:
   ❁ What techniques helped you make your measurements?
   ❁ Which fruit was the longest? Shortest?
   ❁ How many items had measurements that were about halfway between two numbers?
   ❁ What are some true statements about the circumferences?
   ❁ How might looking at length and circumference be useful to farmers? [help estimate the average size of the harvest]
   ❁ What are some things around your home you could measure in this way?

Measurements	Length inches	Circumference inches
eggplant	13 in.	9 in.
cucumber	11 in.	6 in.
carrot	7 in.	1½ in.
zucchini	15 in.	8 in.
fava bean	12 in.	2 in.
tomato	5 in.	11 in.

More Math in the Garden

Finding Mean and Median Have the children arrange all the fruits harvested in a line from shortest to longest and identify the fruit that falls in the middle. This is the median. Older children can graph the data and identify the mean (average) and median for the lengths of fruit.

Comparing the Harvest Youth can compare the measurements of each kind of fruit, identifying the range of data, calculating the average length and circumference, and computing the volume of the items.

Plant Study — Measuring Growth

Ages 8-13

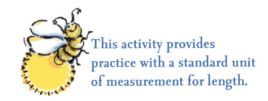

This activity provides practice with a standard unit of measurement for length.

Youth select and draw their favorite plant in the garden. They take and record its measurements and over several weeks check it for changes. Measurement and data collection over time have been used throughout human history by farmers and traditional healers to select wild plant species for food crops and medicines.

What You Need

For Each Pair
- 1 to 2 yards of string
- ruler (inches or centimeters)
- journals
- pencils and crayons

For the Group
- databoard
    - plant sketch
    - "Plant Study Chart — Measurements"
    - "Plant Study Questions"
- colored marking pens
- several yardsticks or meter sticks

Getting Ready

1. Choose a plant in the garden to use for demonstrating measurement techniques, and make a sketch for the databoard. Title two more databoard papers "Plant Study Chart" and "Plant Study Questions."

2. You may want to have youth make their own measuring tool by using a permanent pen and a ruler to mark the length of string in centimeters or inches.

64   MATH IN THE GARDEN

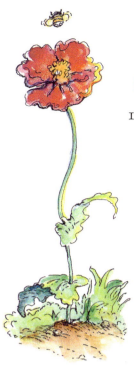

Here We Go

1. Encourage volunteers to describe some of their favorite plants in the garden and why they like them. Point out that for centuries, botanists have grown plants for food, medicine, fiber, and beauty. Making accurate measurements enabled them to analyze the results of their experiments.

2. Tell youth that they will select favorite plants to study that must be no taller in height than a yardstick or meter stick, to ensure that the plant is accessible for study.

3. Hold up a yardstick or meter stick and ask youth to estimate where that height would fall on their bodies. Place the stick up to each and have youth confirm the height's actual location on them. Tell them this will be a useful tool as they choose their plants.

Demonstrating Measuring

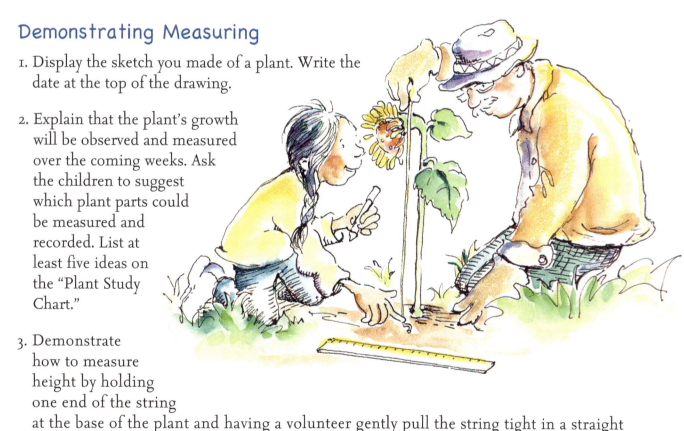

1. Display the sketch you made of a plant. Write the date at the top of the drawing.

2. Explain that the plant's growth will be observed and measured over the coming weeks. Ask the children to suggest which plant parts could be measured and recorded. List at least five ideas on the "Plant Study Chart."

3. Demonstrate how to measure height by holding one end of the string at the base of the plant and having a volunteer gently pull the string tight in a straight line to the top of the plant's stem. As the volunteer holds the string at the top of the stem, let go of your end. Mark the plant length on the string with a crayon or marker.

4. Hold the string up, and have the group silently estimate the height of the plant. Lay the string on the ground in a straight line, and measure its length with a yardstick or meter stick.

MATH IN THE GARDEN

5. Record the length on your plant sketch, noting the units (centimeters or inches), and tell everyone they will record measurements of their own plants in their journals.

6. Encourage the youth to take other measurements in addition to those listed on the "Plant Study Chart." If they want to work with a friend, they need to agree on which plant to study over the next few weeks.

Recording and Discussing Day 1 Observations

1. Distribute the journals and measuring tools, and send the children off to sketch and measure their plants.

2. Assist individuals with measuring as needed. Have the "Plant Study Chart" with you in case some children need help thinking of additional parts to measure. Make sure they are recording measurements accurately and drawing their plants in detail.

3. After about 15 minutes, gather everyone to report plant measurements. Ask volunteers to share interesting features and measurements they have discovered for their plants.

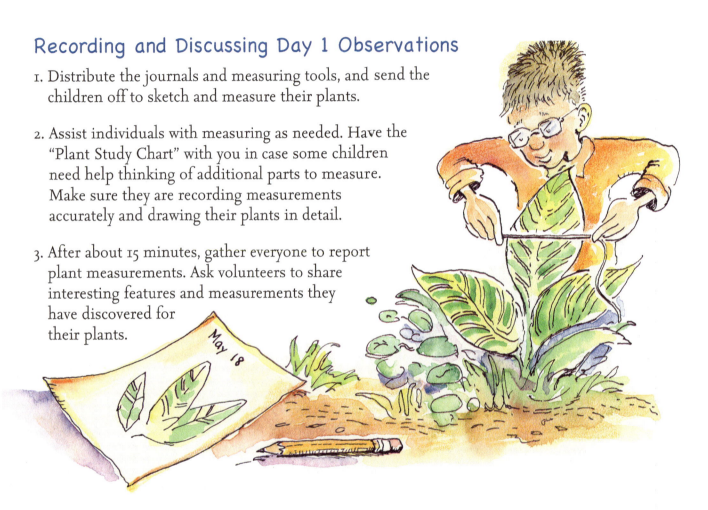

4. Have them look at their measurements to see how they compare. For example, one child might report a 2-foot-high plant. Ask if anyone else had a plant 2 feet high. Then ask:
   ❀ How many had plants that were shorter? How much shorter?
   ❀ How many had plants that were taller? How much taller?
   ❀ What was the tallest plant? What was the shortest?

5. As individuals report a measurement, continue the comparison questions. Add any new measurement categories to the "Plant Study Chart."

Planning and Conducting a Plant Study

1. Ask the youth to predict how their plants will change in a week. After they have discussed their predictions, ask them to pose math questions they would like to investigate. Write their ideas on the "Plant Study Questions" databoard.

2. If they are having difficulty posing math questions that can be investigated, these sample questions may help get them started:

   ❀ How many inches, or centimeters, taller will my plant grow each week?
   ❀ As my plant grows, how much wider does it get?
   ❀ What grows faster, the leaves' length or the stem's height?

3. Ask them to select and record at least two questions they want to use in their plant study.

4. Provide a time frame over the next several weeks in which they will revisit their plants to collect data for their study.

5. At the end of the Plant Study period, you and the children will re-examine their guiding questions and discuss the results.

More Math in the Garden

Graphing Growth Rates Show the youth how to graph length measurements over time to determine which plant parts are changing the most.

Comparing Ratios of Plant Growth Invite youth to determine the ratio of leaf growth to stem growth for different plants.

Measuring with Steps

Ages 5-13

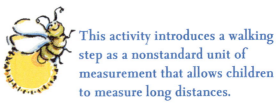

This activity introduces a walking step as a nonstandard unit of measurement that allows children to measure long distances.

Youth measure distances in the garden by counting and recording their steps. Their "counting with steps" method is a useful nonstandard measure used worldwide by gardeners, farmers, builders, and families.

What You Need

For Each Child
- journal
- pencil

For the Group
- databoard
  – "Garden Path" drawing
- yardstick or meter stick
- nonstandard measurement tools, such as string or rope

Getting Ready

On the databoard draw two garden locations and connect them with a pathway that has a clear beginning point and a clear ending point. Label its distance with your number of steps. For example, draw the entrance path from the gate to the student gathering area and label its distance with the number of steps you counted.

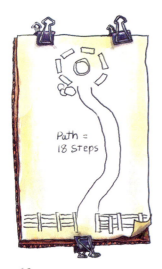

MATH IN THE GARDEN

Here We Go

1. Gather the group in a central garden spot. Ask youth to look around for some long distances within the garden. Listen to their ideas and determine some of the longest distances suggested.

2. Ask youth how the longest distance could be measured.

3. Discuss measuring tools and units that could be used to measure long distances, and the advantages and disadvantages of each. For example, the inch is so small it would be a very time-consuming unit of measurement for a long distance.

4. Show some nonstandard measurement methods, such as string, rope, fingers, and hands. Ask if these would be helpful in measuring distances.

Counting Your Steps

1. Demonstrate a normal walking step, which is a nonstandard unit of measurement. Explain that the step must be a comfortable length since we will be using it over and over to measure out our distances. Contrast a walking step with a "heel to toe" step, which takes more time and is more difficult to perform.

2. Give children a few minutes to practice walking with a comfortable step. In partners, have them walk in lines from the group gathering spot to another identified point. One partner steps, and the other counts the steps. When partners walk back, they change roles of "counter" and "stepper."

3. As they practice, check that everyone understands how to count a step. Did everyone count the same number of steps? Invite them to explain why the step counts vary. [different people have a different length of step; step counters may make mistakes; not everyone started at exactly the same spot]

4. Ask children to suggest some distances in the garden that are suited to this way of measuring. [the distance between beds, to and from the garden shed, from the pond to the greenhouse]

5. Show the group the sample drawing on the databoard of the garden path and its distance measured in your steps.

MATH IN THE GARDEN

Stepping Out

1. Invite partners to choose a location in the garden to measure in steps. They may want to measure the distance around something, such as a garden bed, planter, or building.

2. Have them sketch the pathway they will be measuring in their journals and label the beginning and ending points.

3. Check that partners take turns being the counter/recorder and the stepper. Remind them to record the number of steps they each took.

Recording and Discussing the Data

1. Record their measurements on the group data sheet. Include the description of the distance measured [around the outside of the tool shed] and the number of steps [18 steps].

2. Have youth make observations about the data. Check for distances that were the same or nearly the same. Ask:
   ❀ What was the longest distance? Shortest distance?

3. Discuss how this method is useful. [You don't have to carry a measuring tool; you can measure and travel the distance at the same time.]

4. Ask how knowing these distances might help us in the garden? [knowing how far we would have to push the wheelbarrow to move tools or plants to a garden location; giving directions to someone visiting the garden]

More Math in the Garden

Converting Steps Older children determine the average length of their step in standard units such as inches and feet, or centimeters and decimeters.

Mapping the Garden Youth combine data to generate a map of garden distances in steps or standard units. They illustrate the garden map to make it a clear and useful reference for garden visitors.

New Stepping Out Children use this measuring experience to estimate in steps the distances between other areas of their school grounds and home. Older children convert their step data to standard units of measurement.

How Much Space Does it Take?

Ages 5-13

This activity explores volume using consistent nonstandard units of measurement.

How much space does a potato or tulip bulb take up in the ground? To find out, children cover root vegetables in a container with measured dry sand to determine the volume the plants would occupy underground. This activity gives children direct experience in measuring volume and leads to real-life applications that farmers and families use.

What You Need

For Each Pair
- ¾ gallon dry sand
- gallon container
- 2 pint-sized containers
- 2 identical measuring scoops
- 2 craft sticks
- journals
- pencils

For the Group
- 12 or more bulbs or root vegetables
- 2 databoards
    - "Volume Measuring Steps"
    - "Volume Measurement" chart
- colored marking pens

MATH IN THE GARDEN

Getting Ready

1. Collect containers such as cottage cheese tubs and plastic storage boxes that are large enough to contain a root vegetable with a little room to spare.

2. Get identical measuring scoops, such as coffee scoops or film canisters.

3. Gather a variety of vegetables or bulbs that grow underground, such as potatoes, carrots, radishes, and onions. They must easily and completely fit within the small containers. Remove leafy tops, if necessary.

4. Make two databoards (see the illustrations on pages 73 and 74).

5. Put a vegetable in a container, then fill the container with sand.

Here We Go

1. Show the group the root vegetables and ask children to arrange them by the amount of space they would take up underground.

2. Show children the container filled with sand. Pull out the vegetable and ask:
   ❀ How can we find out how much space a vegetable occupies underground?

3. After listening to their ideas, tell them you have a method to determine the amount of space that is taken up by the vegetable.

4. Fill a measuring scoop with sand and level the surface with a craft stick. Have youth predict, silently to themselves, the number of scoops it will take to fill an empty container.

5. Fill the container, scoop by scoop, as children count along with you. Ask:
   ❈ How many scoops were needed to fill the container?
   ❈ How did the number of scoops compare with your estimate?

6. Explain that all the space inside the container is called the volume. Record the number of scoops needed to fill the volume of the container in column A on the chart. Pour out the sand.

Demonstrating Measurement

1. Hold up a level scoop of sand and a vegetable, side by side. Invite children to estimate how many scoops the vegetable will take up when it is placed in the container.

2. Put the vegetable in the container, then scoop enough sand to fill the container completely to a level surface, as children count with you. Record the number on the chart in column B.

3. Remove the vegetable from the container. Ask:
   ❈ What happened to the level of the sand? Point out that the space the vegetable took up is now empty.

4. Scoop by scoop, add sand until the container is full again. Ask:
   ❈ How many scoops were added? Record the number on the chart in column C.

5. Ask:
   ❈ How can we find out how much space the vegetable took up in the volume of the container?
   Guide their thinking:
   ❈ How many scoops filled the empty container?
   ❈ How many scoops filled the container with the vegetable?
   ❈ What is the difference between the number of scoops?
   ❈ How many scoops equals the space the vegetable took up?

MATH IN THE GARDEN

6. Review the three columns on the chart, and show how subtracting column B from column A equals column C. Tell them that to find the number of scoops the vegetable takes up, they can simply count out scoops for columns A and B and use the math shortcut of subtraction to get data for column C. Record the subtraction in column C.

Measuring Volume

1. Review steps to measure the volume of a vegetable.

2. Divide the group into pairs and let them choose a vegetable to measure. Have them begin measuring and recording their measurements.

3. Circulate among the pairs and check to make certain they understand that the space left in the container is the same as the space taken up by the vegetable when it was covered with sand. As the children remove their vegetable, and the level of the sand drops in the container, have them explain what happened. Ask:
   ❦ What will happen if you bury the vegetable again?
   ❦ What will happen to the sand in the container?

4. Let the youth measure as many vegetables as time allows.

5. Ask questions:
   ❦ What techniques helped you make your measurements?
   ❦ Which vegetables had the largest volume? The smallest?
   ❦ How do the measurements for the same kind of vegetable compare?
   ❦ How would knowing the volume of a vegetable help a gardener? [knowing how far apart to plant or weed it, estimating how much food will be grown, deciding what size box to pack a harvest, what size jar for canning]

6. Ask youth to record their ideas in their journals.

More Math in the Garden

Determining Standard Measurements Have children measure the volume of various scoops, containers, and vegetables using standard units of measurement, such as a quarter cup or a tablespoon. They can record the volume of each container and scoop for use in future activities.

Converting Nonstandard Measurements Older children can convert their nonstandard measurements to standard measures of volume.

Mud Shakes

Ages 5-8

This activity introduces estimating and measuring volume with nonstandard units.

Children compare garden soil to a commercial potting mix. They measure equal volumes of the two soils, measure and add an equal volume of water to each soil, shake it all up, and describe what happens when each soil sample mixes with water. Children learn to be garden scientists as they carry out their soil tests and discuss their results.

What You Need

For Each Pair
- clear plastic jar with lid, 8 to 24 ounces
- stirring stick
- measuring scoop (same for each pair)
- journals
- pencils and crayons

For the Group
- databoard
  - "Mud Shake Recipe"
  - "Mud Shake Tests"
- colored marking pens
- container of commercial garden mix
- small container of garden soil
- bucket of water
- several fine-tip black permanent marking pens

MATH IN THE GARDEN

Getting Ready

1. Identify an area of the garden with flat surfaces where the Mud Shakes can settle.

2. Collect clear plastic jars with lids that are all the same size — small peanut butter jars work well. Using a black permanent marking pen, make an even black line around the top of each jar, a half-inch from the top. A rubber band works well as a guide.

3. Gather the materials, including measuring scoops of the same kind — film canisters work well.

4. Label the databoards "Mud Shake Recipe" and "Mud Shake Tests."

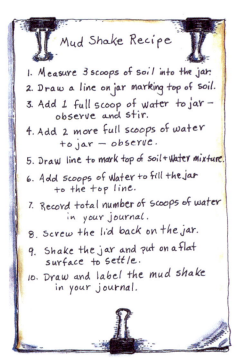

Here We Go

1. Ask children to describe some of the things they have seen in soil. Have one or two volunteers share their ideas about why soil is important.

2. Pass around the container of garden soil, telling children to take a pinch and put it in the palm of one hand. Encourage them to describe how it feels and looks. Do the same with the commercial mix, explaining that it is manufactured from various ingredients.

3. Ask volunteers to describe how the two soils are different and similar. Point out that they will be working as "garden scientists" to compare the properties of garden soil and a commercial mix when water is added, such as during a rainstorm.

Demonstrating a Mud Shake

1. Refer to the "Mud Shake Recipe" as you demonstrate how to measure the commercial garden mix with a scoop.

2. Show them how to level each scoop, and have the children count with you as you add three scoops of soil to a jar. Use the black permanent marking pen to make a line on the jar at the level of the soil.

3. Tell them you will add three equal scoops of water to the jar, one at a time. Ask volunteers to predict the new level of the soil and water and to explain their reasoning. (Some

may predict that the new level will be twice as high because three more scoops will be added; others may predict that the water will "sink into the soil" causing no change in level. The outcome will depend on the nature of the commercial soil you use.)

4. Add one scoop of water and let the children observe the mixed soil and water level. Have them revise their predictions based on what they see. With each added scoop of water, a volunteer can stir and then describe the mixture. Ask:
   ❀ Does the water sink into the soil or form little puddles until mixed?
   ❀ How has the color of the soil changed?

5. After three equal scoops of soil and of water have been added and mixed in the jar, mark the "soil + water" level with a pen. Tap the jar to level the soil surface.

6. Direct children to silently predict how many scoops of water must be added to fill the jar up to the top black line. Have them count with you as you add water, and describe what they see, until the water level reaches the line. Record the total number of water scoops on the "Mud Shake Tests" chart.

7. Replace the lid on the jar and have a volunteer shake the soil mixture well. Place the Mud Shake on a stable surface to settle for a few minutes, while you divide the group into pairs and have them draw the results of the Commercial Mix Mud Shake in their journals.

Making Garden Soil Mud Shakes

1. Review the steps for making a Mud Shake to test the garden soil. Encourage the children to take turns counting, measuring, and recording their results. They can use crayons to show the soil colors. Remind them to avoid moving their Mud Shake once it has begun to settle. Tell them they need to find a spot nearby to collect their scoops of garden soil.

2. As you circulate among the garden scientists, ask:
   ❀ What happened when you added water to the soil?
   ❀ How do the levels for 3 scoops of soil and 3 scoops of water compare?
   ❀ How many scoops of water did it take to fill the jar?

MATH IN THE GARDEN

3. While waiting for the mixtures to settle, pairs should describe their observations and draw and write them in their journals. They should also note where they got the soil. [near the gate, by the sunflower, in the bean bed] They will see such things as the water turning dark, foam and bits of materials floating to the top, pebbles and sand settling to the bottom, and layers of fine silt and clay settling last. Ask:
   ❀ How is your Mud Shake similar to the commercial mix?
   ❀ What do you see in the floating layer? [leaves, twigs, bark]
   ❀ What has settled to the bottom? [rocks, sand, silt, clay]

Most soil organisms are desirable and harmless. If small animals are discovered floating in the mud shake, after quickly taking the measurements, instruct pairs to pour the sample back into the garden.

4. Explain that the material floating to the top of the jar is mostly organic matter composed of things like leaves and bark. Organic matter helps soil retain moisture and provides important nutrients to plants. Ask:
   ❀ Which soil contains the most organic matter?
   ❀ In what other ways do the Mud Shakes differ?

Analyzing the Results

1. Gather the group and ask children to report their findings.
   ❀ How did the Commercial Mix and Garden Soil samples differ?
   ❀ How many scoops of water were added to each sample?
   ❀ Which sample has the thickest layer of rocks and sand on the bottom? Where did it come from?
   ❀ Which sample has the thickest layer floating at the top?
   ❀ How many layers of different material did you find at the bottom of each sample?

2. While observing the children at work, identify potential volunteers to call on who have recorded their measurements and observations.

3. Have the children record in their journals one or two questions that were sparked by their investigations. Encourage children to share the things they would like to learn more about.

More Math in the Garden

Measuring the Layers Older children can use rulers to measure and record the sizes of the various layers of soil, water, and floating material.

Mud Marble Test Have children squeeze and roll small 1-inch "marbles" from a sample of each moistened soil. If the soil is high in nutrient-rich clay, the ball will hold its shape when dried. Children can compare different soils using the marble test.

Weighing the Garden Harvest

Ages 5-13

Merchants and farmers have used both nonstandard and standard measures for centuries. This activity gives children an opportunity to create their own weights and use them to compare fruits and vegetables using a balance scale.

What You Need

For Each Team of Four
- 10 or more identical watertight plastic containers (e.g., water bottles, film canisters with lids, spice jars, modeling clay containers)
- small bucket of water
- several fruits and vegetables
- balance scale
- journals
- pencils

For the Group
- databoard
- colored marking pens
- extra identical water-tight plastic containers

Getting Ready

1. If you do not already have balance scales, see the instructions on the following page to make your own. Identify places in the garden where you can hang the balance scales, such as hooks or low-hanging branches.

2. Tight-sealing plastic containers can be used as uniform nonstandard weights.

This activity introduces weight using a consistent nonstandard unit to compare objects.

MATH IN THE GARDEN

How to Make a Balance Scale

What You Need

- plastic coat hanger with metal swivel hook
- two 6-cup plastic food storage containers
- four 18-inch pieces of string
- 12-inch piece of string
- heavy washer or other similar weight
- hand drill

Making a Balance Scale

1. Drill or bore a small hole in each corner of the plastic containers. Take one 18" string and thread each end through two adjacent holes, securing each end with a knot. Thread another string similarly on the opposite side so the strings are relatively even in length. Do the same for the second container.

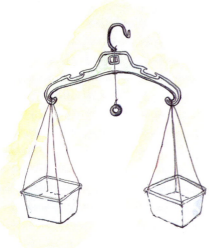

2. Some plastic hangers have hooks at the very ends that can be used to support the strings and plastic containers. If the hanger lacks end hooks, use a power hand drill to make a hole at each end of the hanger. Put the open end of a paper clip through each hole to create a hook for the hanging containers.

3. Make a plumb line by tying a heavy washer to one end of the 12" string and tying the other end to the middle of the hanger, at the hook. Test to see if the containers are even and balanced. Adjust as necessary.

4. Practice using the balance scale. In one container, place the object you want to weigh. In the other container, add weights, one or two at a time, until the plumb line is on the midpoint and the containers are balanced.

You can repurpose containers such as old water bottles, film canisters with lids, spice jars, and modeling clay containers. To work properly, containers must be identical in size and composition. The number you will need depends on your group size. Opaque containers can be used for full weights, but clear containers are needed if you want to use fractional weights such as ½ and ¼.

3. Gather a variety of fruits and vegetables, such as bell peppers, lemons, potatoes, pattypan squash, and onions. Include a range of sizes, shapes, and densities to spark interest.

Here We Go

1. Display the produce and ask for comments about it.
   - Which one do you predict is the heaviest?
   - Which one do you predict is the lightest?
   - Which items do you think are about the same weight?

2. Pass the produce around to allow everyone to feel and talk about the weights of the various items and revise their predictions. Point out that each person senses weight differently.

3. Explain that grocery stores usually sell produce by a standard unit known as a pound. Tell them they are going to weigh the produce without a grocery store scale; instead they will use a balance scale and weights that they make. Let the children suggest how the balance scale works, and help a volunteer demonstrate the balancing action.

4. Draw their attention to the plumb line (the string and washer hung in the middle) and how it hangs down straight when the two baskets are equal in weight.

5. Demonstrate how to make water weights for the balance scales. Fill a water-tight plastic container by holding it underwater and replacing the lid. This will minimize air bubbles and ensure that all canisters are filled to the same level. Tell youth to make a half-weight and a quarter-weight to use in the balance scale.

6. Divide the group into teams of four and have each team fill plastic containers and create their weighing units.

Fruit/Veggie	Number of Canisters
tomato	2
radish	1
lemon	4
potato	7
apple	5

Using the Balance Scale

1. Demonstrate how to weigh a fruit or vegetable in the balance scale using the plastic containers of water as the uniform nonstandard unit of weight.

2. Let the children predict how many containers they think their fruit or vegetable will weigh. Have them weigh it, adding as many containers as they need, until the baskets on the balance scale are level.

3. Youth may need to use a fractional unit to make the balance scale even. Have them estimate the water level in the container. Is it about $1/4$, $1/3$, $1/2$, or $3/4$?

4. Have the children record their produce and its weight on the databoard and in their journals.

5. When teams have finished weighing their produce and recording on the databoard, gather the group for a discussion of the results. Ask questions to guide true statements about the weight of each item:
   * Which fruit or vegetable weighed the most?
   * Which weighed the least?
   * How did the balance scale results compare with your predictions?
   * How could you check to see if two fruits or vegetables that weighed the same number of containers are equal in weight? [put one in each basket]
   * How do "standard" weights make it easier for both farmers and buyers? [they know more accurately how much is being bought and sold]

More Math in the Garden

Produce Line Up Have the children line up the produce by weight from the lightest to the heaviest. With older children, discuss why the size of an item might not reflect its amount of weight. Cut open and reveal interiors of some choice items.

Produce Price Have the children assign a price per container that the produce could cost. If all the fruits and vegetables were sold at this same price per container, how much would each cost? Have them make a cost column in their journals, and add this to the databoard.

CHAPTER THREE
Geometry & Pattern

Everything has shape and dimension, and those attributes help to define objects. Geometry and pattern prevail in all forms of everyday life and have been used by cultures worldwide from ancient to modern times. Children's first experiences with geometry are informal and organic in nature — arising from discovery about the world around them. From experiences with objects, they learn to name common two-dimensional shapes in context and develop an understanding of how things fit together.

Formally, geometry is the study of points, lines, angles, planes, and space. Geometry provides the language to describe the objects in the world and the relationships among them. Plane geometry is the study of shapes and figures in two dimensions — the plane. Plane figures only have length and width. The common plane shapes include circles, triangles, squares, rectangles, and hexagons. Three-dimensional shapes are called polyhedrons (or polyhedra) and have height in addition to length and width. Common examples include cubes, cylinders, and pyramids. In the garden, planter boxes and barrels are examples of polyhedrons.

Geometric concepts encompass relationships among shapes and forms. A pattern is a special type of relationship — it is found in anything that repeats itself over and over again. Though never perfect in nature, patterns abound and include spirals, branching, and symmetry. In the garden, there are many opportunities to explore and learn more about geometry. The activities in this section involve investigations to introduce and deepen understanding of patterns, angles, two-dimensional shapes, area, perimeter, and symmetry.

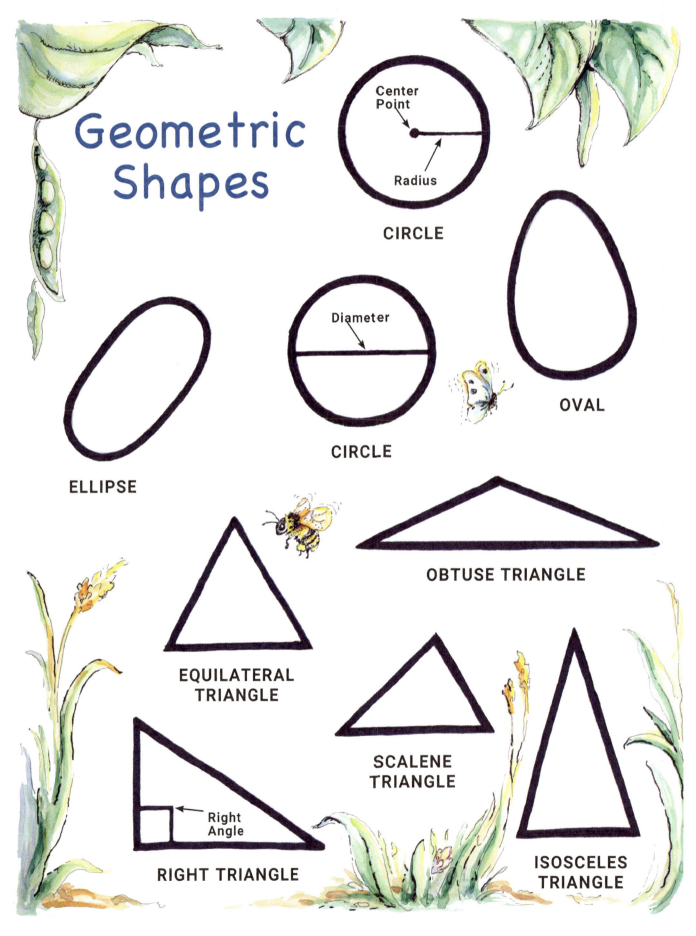

Cross Cut Snacks

Ages 5-13

This activity explores attributes of geometric shapes.

Youth are encouraged to taste vegetables and fruits that are new to them while exploring foods that are cut and arranged to display a variety of geometric shapes. They classify the different snack items according to geometric shapes. They draw and label the shapes and assemble nutritious snack items to produce a design that they then will eat.

What You Need

For Each Person
- paper plate
- napkin
- journal
- pencil and crayons

For the Group
- "Geometric Shapes" illustration on pages 84 and 85
- 4 to 6 different kinds of produce, at least two of each
- knife
- cutting board
- serving implements and containers
- databoard
  – "Shape List" chart
- colored marking pens
- paper for labels

Getting Ready

1. Slice and prepare the food items to exhibit a variety of geometric shapes, leaving one of each kind whole to display. As you cut different shapes, sort them into separate containers — one shape per

86　　MATH IN THE GARDEN

container. One shape may be made from several different foods. (Triangles can be cut out of zucchini, jicama, and cucumbers.) The "Geometric Shapes" illustration on the preceding pages provides ideas for a variety of closed curved shapes and polygons, and can be displayed with the food to help the children identify and name the shapes. Food choices you can use to make diverse shapes include:

- **sphere, hemisphere:** tomato, cherry, blueberry, pea
- **cylinder, circle, oval:** carrot, bean, grape, banana, cucumber, zucchini, orange
- **half-circle:** celery, daikon, radish, apple
- **various 4-sided shapes** (square, rectangle): celery, cucumber, zucchini, jicama
- **other polygons:** cucumber, zucchini, jicama, starfruit

2. Arrange the shape plates in a line that can be viewed easily by the group and sampled in a buffet style.

3. Cut the paper to make labels for the shape on each plate.

4. Place the uncut fruit or vegetable among the prepared foods as additional examples of natural shapes.

5. On the databoard, make a "Shape List" chart of the geometric shapes you cut from the foods.

Here We Go

1. Gather the children where they can all view the buffet-style snack items and the "Geometric Shapes" illustration (pages 84 and 85). Ask volunteers to name the shapes and place the labels next to them as they are identified.

2. Invite children to observe and identify the foods they see that have been cut into different shapes. Some foods may have been cut into two or more geometric shapes.

3. Explain that a goal of the activity is to explore geometric shapes and encourage each other to try out some new foods. Each person will create a geometric design on a plate using a selection of the foods. They will draw the shapes in their journals while eating the snack.

4. Have the children suggest how they will share the food fairly and post their guidelines. [take only one or two of the snacks until everyone has made their selection; if you touch it, you must eat it; ask leader before taking seconds]

5. Suggest that they each take a few shape pieces to snack on while they are creating their geometric designs. Distribute journals so they can make a record of their shapes and designs.

Looking for Shapes

1. Encourage the children to taste at least one food that is new to them or that they seldom eat.

2. Circulate among the children, observing their responses and conversations. Congratulate those who have been adventurous in tasting new foods.

3. The following questions may be useful in assessing prior knowledge and stimulating discussion:
    ❋ How many foods did you choose that were cut into the same shape?

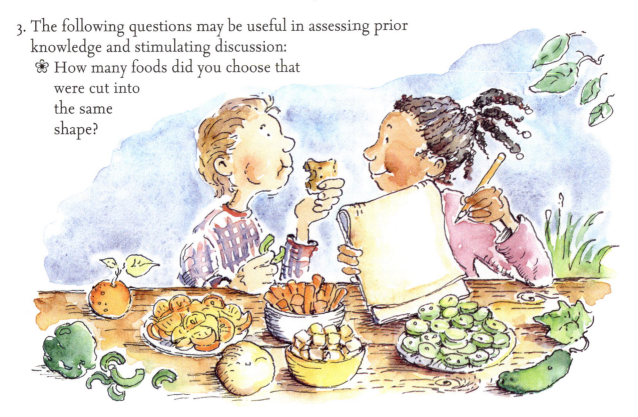

   ❋ How many different shapes are you using?
   ❋ How does the shape of a cucumber change depending on how you look at it? From the end? From the side?
   ❋ What new food did you try?
   ❋ How do your food choices differ from your neighbor's?
   ❋ What shapes did you combine to make new shapes for your design?

4. After about 10 minutes, direct everyone to put the finishing touches on their designs and drawings. Remind them to label their drawings with the names of the geometric shapes they used.

Talking About the Snacks

1. Survey the youth for what shape selections they made. Record these on the "Shape List" chart. Ask:
   - How did your predictions compare with the results?
   - What shape was eaten by the most people? The least?

2. Encourage volunteers to share their drawings of geometric shapes and snack experiences. The following questions may be useful in stimulating their feedback:
   - How many different kinds of 4-sided shapes did you find?
   - What strategies can you use to make a new geometric shape for your design? [stack two items, lay two side by side]
   - Were some foods of the same shape eaten more than others of that same shape? Why do you think some foods were eaten less?
   - How many people tried eating a new food?
   - What helped you decide to try a new food?
   - What will you tell your friends about geometric snacks?

3. Invite everyone to reflect on trying new foods and write their thoughts in their journals.

More Math in the Garden

Creating New Shapes Invite youth to cut the fresh fruit and vegetables into different geometric shapes.

Making More Pattern Snacks Repeat this activity again when you have snacks with your group and note how preferences and the use of shapes change.

Shapes in the Garden

Ages 5-8

Children search for a variety of shapes in vegetation and garden structures. By drawing the shapes they find, children develop an understanding of the characteristics and properties of geometric shapes.

This activity explores attributes of geometric shapes.

What You Need

For Each Pair
- journals
- pencils and crayons

For the Group
- databoard
  – 3 to 4 pieces of paper
- "Geometric Shapes" illustration on pages 84 and 85
- colored marking pens

Getting Ready

Visit the garden in advance to identify the best areas for children to conduct their "shape hunt."

Here We Go

1. Gather the group in the garden, and tell the children they are going on a "shape hunt." Before they do, ask them what shapes they know.

90 MATH IN THE GARDEN

2. As children suggest shapes, have them sketch the shape on the databoard, and encourage volunteers to name the shapes and describe the attributes. [triangle has three sides and three angles; square has four sides and four right angles]

3. Show them the "Geometric Shapes" illustration (pages 84 and 85) and suggest that these same shapes can be found all around them in both natural and human-made objects in the garden.

4. Demonstrate looking closely for angles in a nearby plant and point out the shapes revealed in leaves, flowers, fruits, and stems.

5. Distribute the journals and direct the children to find as many shapes as they can, and to sketch at least 6 different shapes in their journals.

6. Send them off in pairs to explore the garden. Remind them to observe things that are at all levels in the garden, from up in trees to below their feet.

Sharing Shapes

1. When all pairs have returned with their sketches, gather the group in a circle. Ask what shapes they found. As they suggest a shape, such as an oval or ellipse, refer to your "Geometric Shapes" illustration and review its attributes.

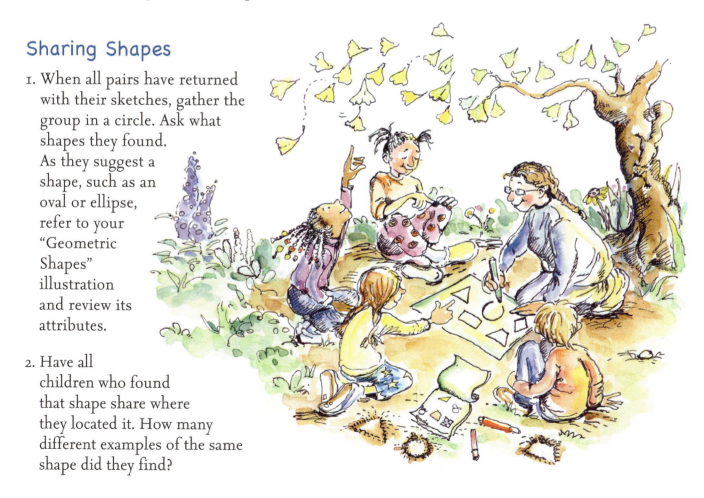

2. Have all children who found that shape share where they located it. How many different examples of the same shape did they find?

MATH IN THE GARDEN

3. Continue until every child has contributed at least one shape. Ask:
   ❦ Which shapes did we find?
   ❦ Which shape was the easiest to find?

Hunting for Shapes Again

1. Have children go on a second "shape hunt" to find ones that were not found during the earlier search, or to give them a few unusual shapes to locate.

2. Use a few of the following kinds of questions to help focus observations on shape attributes:
   ❦ How many sides does the triangle have? [3]
   ❦ What do we call this space where two lines meet in a triangle? [angle; "tri" in triangle means 3]
   ❦ How many sides does the rectangle have? [4]
   ❦ What can we say about the angles where the lines meet on the rectangle? [they look like the capital letter L; are 90°; are right angles]
   ❦ How many sides does a diamond (rhombus) have? [4]
   ❦ What can we say about the angles in a diamond? [2 small angles and 2 large angles; the small angles are equal; the large angles are equal]

Carpenters named a 90° angle a "right" angle — a table made with right angles is sturdy and will stay "upright."

More Math in the Garden

Geometric Snacks During a snack break, provide a variety of fruits and vegetables and invite children to identify geometric shapes.

Collecting Shapes Children help create a geometric-shape chart to display leaf and flower collections and drawings of natural geometric shapes from the garden.

The Great Triangle Hunt

Ages 5–13

Youth look for triangular shapes in the garden. Younger children focus on the sides of triangles, and older ones focus on angles within triangles. In nature, geometric shapes are not perfect, yet in the garden one can find many shapes that closely approximate triangles.

This activity explores attributes of triangles and angles.

What You Need

For Each Team of Three
- 6-foot length of string
- 3" x 5" index card
- journals
- pencils

For the Group
- databoard
  – several sheets of paper
- colored marking pens
- "Kinds of Triangles" illustration on page 95

Getting Ready

1. Tie the ends of each 6-foot length of string together to make loops.

2. In the garden, identify a triangular object to use at the start of the "Triangle Hunt."

Here We Go

1. Have several volunteers draw triangles on the databoard. Encourage the children to describe what makes them triangles.

MATH IN THE GARDEN

93

2. Place another sheet of paper on the databoard, and draw a line everyone can see. With the group helping, create a triangle and define it. [closed shape with three sides and three angles]

3. Select two individuals to be your partners to demonstrate how to use the string loop to create a triangle. Assign yourself and each volunteer a different place on the string. Each person gently pulls on the loop to form three straight lines.

4. Divide the group into teams of three and give each group a string loop to make their own triangle. Encourage them to experiment with the loop to form different triangles.

Where two sides of a triangle meet an angle is formed.

5. Have them identify each of the three sides and three angles in their triangles.

6. Hold up the "Kinds of Triangles" illustration on the following page and have the youth create each example with their string loops: equilateral triangle, isosceles triangle, scalene triangle, right triangle, and obtuse triangle.

Hunting for Triangles

1. Distribute journals and pencils to the group. Take them near the triangular object in the garden you selected earlier. Describe the characteristics of your triangular object, and encourage the youth to find it. For example: it has two equal sides and one short side; it has three small angles; it is blue.

2. Invite them to point out what features make it a triangle. Have the children sketch this triangle in their journals and label where it was found. [branch of a tree, lattice fence, petal of a flower]

3. For children ages 5-8, tell teams to find and draw in their journals at least three more examples of triangles and note where they found each one.

    For youth ages 8-13, tell teams to find, draw, and label in their journals one of each of the following kinds of triangles: equilateral, isosceles, scalene, right, and obtuse.

4. After everyone has completed drawings, call them together.

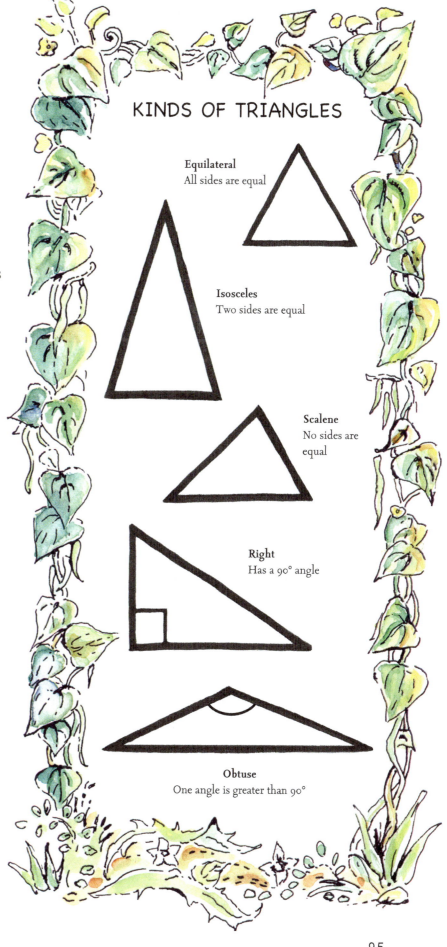

MATH IN THE GARDEN

5. Have the group note the similarities and differences in the triangles they found.

6. Ask questions to review the different types of triangles:

- ❋ Look at the sides on your triangles. How many sides must a triangle have? [3]
- ❋ Show the illustration of an equilateral triangle. Who has a triangle with all three sides almost the same length? Where did you find it?
- ❋ Show the illustration of an isosceles triangle. Who has a triangle with two sides almost the same length? Where did you find it?
- ❋ Show the illustration of a scalene triangle. Who has a triangle with three unequal sides? Where did you find it?
- ❋ Show the illustration of a right triangle. Who found a right triangle? Where did you find it? Where is the right angle in the triangle?

The size of an angle is measured in degrees. The sum of all the angles in a triangle is 180°. Circles help define the degrees in angles:

Circle has 360°.

Half-circle has 180° and contains a straight angle.

Three-quarter circle has 270° and contains an obtuse angle.

Quarter circle has 90° and contains a right angle.

Eighth circle has 45° and contains an acute angle.

For the older teams continue with these questions:
- ❋ Show the illustration of an obtuse triangle. Who has a triangle that contains an obtuse angle? Where is the obtuse angle? Where did you find it? What is the name of the other two angles in this triangle? [acute]

7. Ask the group how they might use different triangular shapes to design a garden. Ask them to draw or write their ideas in their journals.

More Math in the Garden

Planting in Triangles Subdivide a garden bed into various triangular areas and decide which plants would look best in those triangles.

Eating Triangles Prepare snacks that are triangular in shape. Many fruits and vegetables can be cut easily into triangular shapes for children to identify and discuss.

Geometric Windows

Ages 5-8

Children use paper frames of three geometric shapes to observe the small details and patterns of leaves. They compare leaves with parallel veins to those with a netted pattern to develop a sense of the attributes of shapes and of leaves.

This activity reinforces identification of attributes, patterns, and shapes and introduces data collection using samples.

What You Need

For Each Team of Three
- 3 Geometric Windows (triangle, square, and circle; instructions below)
- journals
- pencils

For the Group
- databoard
- colored marking pens
- collection of interesting leaves
- 3 colors of construction paper
- scissors

Getting Ready

1. Make three geometric windows (triangle, square, and circle) for each team of three children. The square and triangle should have 1-inch sides. The circle should have a diameter of 1 inch. Make the windows from 4" x 8" pieces of construction paper folded in half to make

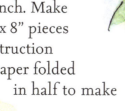

MATH IN THE GARDEN

small 4-inch square folders that will be used to hold the leaves. Choose a different color for each shape. In the center of each folder draw one of the shapes, then cut through both pages to create a geometric window. These 1-inch viewers can be reused many times.

2. Collect several leaves to use in the demonstration. If possible, choose leaves with net-like veins, as well as some with parallel veins. Avoid leaves that are thick, prickly, very large, or very small.

Here We Go

1. Gather the children in the garden. Tell them they will sharpen their observation skills as they take a closer look at leaves from at least two different plants.

2. Show the children the paper geometric windows and ask what the shapes are called. Point out the circle, triangle, and square. Explain that viewing objects with the small geometric windows will help them focus their observations on different leaf attributes and patterns.

3. Demonstrate how to look at leaves using the geometric windows. Put leaves inside windows and have children hold them up to the light. Ask:
   ❦ What features do you see through the shape windows? [veins, hairs, patterns, holes, spots of light]
   ❦ What happens if you rotate the leaf in the frame? [in triangle and square: pattern changes; in circle: pattern stays the same]

Comparing Views

1. Divide the children into teams of three. Tell team members they will take turns using the three geometric windows until each person has used all

three shapes to observe and record what they see. Each person will use a window to view, draw, and label observations of two different leaves. Then children swap their windows and draw the new views until everyone has used the three geometric views. Those who finish early can rotate leaves within windows and make additional drawings.

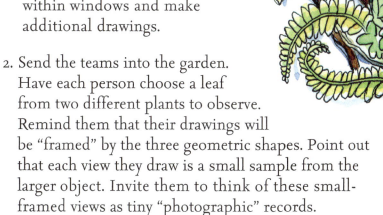

2. Send the teams into the garden. Have each person choose a leaf from two different plants to observe. Remind them that their drawings will be "framed" by the three geometric shapes. Point out that each view they draw is a small sample from the larger object. Invite them to think of these small-framed views as tiny "photographic" records.

3. Circulate among the teams and encourage children to make detailed drawings in their journals. Stimulate their observations as necessary by asking questions such as:
   ❁ What patterns do you see in the leaves?
   ❁ How does the view change if the leaf is rotated?
   ❁ How do the areas inside the framed views compare? Which is largest? Smallest?
   ❁ How much of the leaf have you sampled — less than half of the surface, more than half?
   ❁ How many leaf veins touch the edge of (intersect) each window shape?

Talking About the Small Views

1. Save enough time for the children to share their observations and experiences with the geometric views. Ask questions such as:
   ❊ What features did you notice using different geometric windows?
   ❊ What smaller geometric shapes did you find within the window view?

2. Sketch the three shapes at the top of the databoard and have children tally and compare the data for different views. Ask:
   ❊ How many veins intersected the edges of each of the different shapes?
   ❊ How many insect holes can you see within the different shapes?

3. Who might use small samples like our "windows" to estimate large numbers of objects? [biologist estimating ducks on a lake, cancer researcher estimating number of tumor cells]

4. Who might use small samples to create larger patterns? [computer designer, fabric designer, landscape architect]

5. Ask children to write in their journals about how the different shapes and sizes of the "windows" affected their observations of leaves.

# of Veins Intersecting Edge

	△	○	□
Laurie	11	11	12
William	10	13	15
Isobel	9	10	11
Jamal	6	8	8
Carlos	10	10	10
Kesha	10	13	14

More Math in the Garden

Comparing Journals Have the children lay out their journals for all to see. Put all the leaves from this activity in a basket, and then challenge the children to find the set of drawings that documents each leaf.

Hunting for Shapes Conduct a geometric shape hunt in the garden.

Creating Shapes Use giant string loops to create geometric shapes on the ground to enclose sample plots for weed and insect studies.

Angle Search

Ages 8-13

This activity explores angles of real objects using Craft Stick Calipers to record and compare angles.

Youth identify angles around them by creating angles with their hands, and searching for angles in the garden with calipers. While exploring for angles in the garden, youth categorize angles by their measures.

What You Need

For Each Person
- Craft Stick Calipers (see page 102)
- journal
- pencil

For the Group
- wooden craft sticks
- roll of 2-inch-wide plastic tape
- permanent marking pen, same color as tape
- scissors
- databoard
  – angles chart
- colored marking pens

Getting Ready

Make an angles chart for the databoard with the headings "Narrow Angles (Acute)" and "Wide Angles (Obtuse)." Draw three horizontal lines across the page below. See the illustration on page 104.

MATH IN THE GARDEN

101

How to Make Calipers from Craft Sticks

1. Cut a 1" x 2" piece of plastic tape.

2. Lay two craft sticks, end to end, along the center of the length of tape, leaving a ⅛-inch gap between the sticks (so they may be twisted in a later step).

3. Wrap tape tightly around sticks, preserving the gap.

4. Use a permanent marking pen to color the top side of the sticks. This coloring makes the angles easier to see.

5. Holding one stick flat on a firm surface, twist the other stick 180° so the colored side is face down.

6. Fold one stick 180° over on top of the other. See illustration at right.

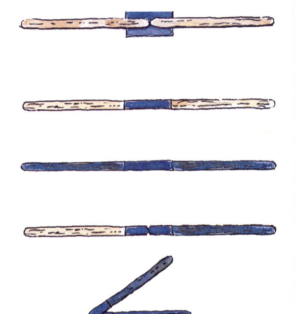

Here We Go

1. Ask the youth to describe a circle and to describe a triangle. Ask:
   ❋ How is a triangle different from a circle? [circle has no corners, triangle has corners and angles]

2. Introduce the word "angle" if someone doesn't bring up the term. When two lines come together and meet at a point, they form an angle.

3. Have youth put their hands together side by side with the tips of their index fingers touching. Show them how to make angles by keeping their fingertips touching and moving the heels of their hands apart.

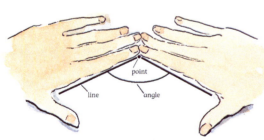

4. Ask the youth to move their hands slowly in or out,

still keeping their fingertips together, to make various angles. Let the youth describe those new angles. [bigger, thinner, wider, narrower]

5. Tell them to look around and spot angles or corners on anything they see — it can be man-made or natural.

Looking for Angles

1. Tell youth that they are going to search for angles in the garden and use a special tool to draw the angle. Ask:
   ❦ Where do you see angles in plants around you? [where stem and leaf meet, leaf veins]

2. Have everyone make an angle using his or her thumb and pointer finger. Go up to a plant and show how you can "copy" the angle by placing your thumb and pointer finger over the plant's angle.

3. Show the youth the Craft Stick Calipers. Place it over the same angle on the plant. By carefully holding that angle shape, relocate the calipers onto the databoard and trace the angle. Label the angle with the plant or object on which it was found. [tomato plant, laurel bush, bench]

4. Let the youth search the garden for angles. When they find one, have them use their calipers to measure it. Then they should draw and label the angle in their journals. Encourage them to find at least four angles of different sizes.

Comparing Angles

1. Gather the group once they have finished and ask:
   ❦ How many found narrow angles? Wide angles? L-shaped angles?
   ❦ Where did you find them?

2. Display the angles chart and explain that the math term for narrow angles (smaller than L-shaped angles) is "acute angle." Have several volunteers use their calipers to duplicate "acute" angles they found on the line below the appropriate math term. Help them position their calipers

MATH IN THE GARDEN

so that the line on the databoard forms the base of the angle. Tell them to draw a small curved arrow to show the width of the angle.

3. Have volunteers use their calipers to draw several examples of "obtuse angles" (greater than L-shaped angles) on the other side of the databoard, identifying the size of the angle with an arrow.

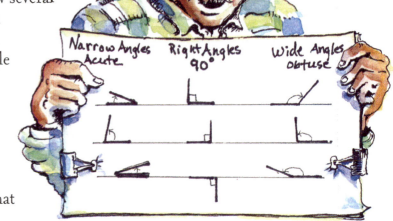

4. Ask the group what units are used to measure angles. [degrees] Introduce the term "right angle" for the L-shaped angle, and draw one on a line in the center of the databoard. Tell the youth that a right angle has 90°.

5. Have volunteers add right angles to the databoard, and show them how adding a small square in the corner where the lines meet denotes a right angle.
    ❈ Which angles measure less than a right angle? [acute angles are less than 90°]
    ❈ Which angles measure more than a right angle? [obtuse angles are more than 90° and less than 180°]

6. Draw a straight line and let the children estimate how many degrees it has. [a straight angle has 180°]

7. Encourage youth to talk about and compare the angles. Some will notice that for each acute angle on a line, there is a subsequent obtuse angle created that forms a straight angle (180°), and vice versa. These are called supplementary angles. Given an acute or obtuse angle's measure, the supplementary angle can be determined.

More Math in the Garden

Measuring with Calipers Have the youth find, draw, and measure angles at home and in their classrooms using the calipers.

Measuring with Protractors Show the youth how to use a protractor, and have them measure their angles in degrees.

Measuring Angles in Garden Plots When working with garden plots in the shape of polygons (triangles, trapezoids, parallelograms) have individuals measure and compare the angles of the plots.

Planting in Circles

Ages 8-13

This activity introduces the radius, diameter, and circumference of circles.

Youth make circular planting beds in the soil and plant flowers to mark the center, the radius, and the diameter of each circle. In the circular beds between the flowers, they plant rapidly growing salad crops.

What You Need

For Each Team of Three to Four
- Radius Measurement Tool (see instructions on page 106)
- 1-meter length of non-stretchy string
- 4 seed packets, each for a different salad crop
- 9 flower seedlings, marigolds are excellent
- journals
- pencils

For the Group
- roll of non-stretchy string
- pencils, 2 per team
- pen or marker
- meter stick
- databoard
    - "Parts of a Circle" chart
    - "Circumference and Radius" chart
- colored marking pens

Getting Ready

1. Pick areas in the garden for several planting circles that are about 60 cm in diameter — about the length of an arm. Have enough space between the planting circles so a team of children can gather around a circle to make a planting bed.

MATH IN THE GARDEN

2. Prepare the soil in the planting areas. It's best if soil is damp, not extremely wet, nor bone dry.

3. Gather seed packets for a variety of salad crops. You will need 4 packets for each team. If you have several teams, make seed-packet bundles for teams for easy distribution during the activity.

4. Make a **Radius Measurement Tool** for each team by tying tiny pencil-sized loops in a 35-cm string at the 0-cm, 15-cm, and 30-cm points along it. Put a pencil in the 0-cm and 15-cm loops of each tool.

5. For each team, cut a 1-meter length of string. For your demonstration, cut two pieces of string — one 1 meter and one 2 meters in length.

6. On the databoard, label one piece of paper "Parts of a Circle" and sketch a circle about the size of a paper plate on it. You will label the parts later in the activity.

7. Draw the "Circumference and Radius" chart as illustrated on page 108 and put it under several pieces of paper for use after your demonstration.

Here We Go

1. Gather the youth at one of the areas where they will make their circular planting beds. Inform them they will plant salad crops in a design of a circle within a circle.

2. Display the "Parts of a Circle" chart and ask the youth what they know about circles. When a part is discussed, draw and label it on your drawing. Help the youth to define a circle, its circumference, its radius, and its diameter.

3. Show the youth a Radius Measurement Tool. Tell them that all parts of a circle need to be an equal distance from the center and this special tool will help them make a circle in the soil. Point out the 0-cm end with a loop, and two other loops, one at 15 cm and one at 30 cm. Make sure that there is a pencil in both the 0-cm and 15-cm loops.

For any circle, there is a direct relationship between the length of the radius and the length of the circumference.

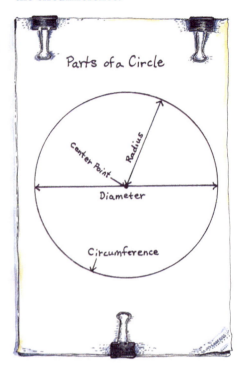

Parts of a Circle

- **Circle** is a two-dimensional figure with all points the same distance from a fixed point, called the center point.
- **Radius** is a straight line from the center point to any point on the circle.
- **Diameter** is a straight line that joins two points on a circle and goes through the center point. It is twice the length of the radius.
- **Circumference** is the distance measured around a circle.

4. Demonstrate how to use the Radius Measurement Tool to make a circle in a planting bed.

   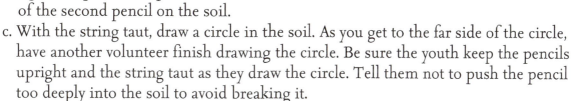

   a. Have a volunteer hold the center-point pencil upright on the soil, keeping it in one spot.
   b. Stretch the string tight and place the tip of the second pencil on the soil.
   c. With the string taut, draw a circle in the soil. As you get to the far side of the circle, have another volunteer finish drawing the circle. Be sure the youth keep the pencils upright and the string taut as they draw the circle. Tell them not to push the pencil too deeply into the soil to avoid breaking it.

   d. Have volunteers deepen the circle line with their fingers. This is the furrow into which they will plant seeds. Ask:
      ❦ What do you call the distance between the two pencils? [radius]
      ❦ What is the length of the radius? [15 cm]
      ❦ What is the length of the diameter? [30 cm]
      ❦ How does it compare to the radius? [diameter = twice the length of radius]

   e. Take the pencil from the 15-cm loop and put it into the 30-cm loop. Keep the center-point pencil in the same spot, while making a larger circle around the first circle.

Comparing Circumferences and Radii

1. Look at the two circles and ask which circle has the greatest circumference for planting. How much bigger is it? Ask for predictions about the difference between the circumferences. Ask how they could compare the lengths. [measure the lengths of the two circumferences]

   a. Have two volunteers lay a 1-meter length of string into the circumference line of the inner circle. Have them mark the circumference length on the string by holding it with their fingers and marking it with a pen.

MATH IN THE GARDEN

b. Invite two more volunteers to lay a 2-meter length of string into the circumference line of the outer circle and mark the circumference length with a pen.

c. Once the measuring is done, ask the volunteers to help you compare circumferences of the circles. For each piece of string have one youth hold the starting point end and another hold the circumference mark. Let the pair holding the ends of each string stand shoulder-to-shoulder while the other two individuals back away until the strings are taut. Ask:

- ❀ Which circle has a bigger circumference? [outer circle]
- ❀ How much bigger? [looks about twice as long]
- ❀ How would you figure it out? [Fold the larger circumference string in half and show that it is the same length as the smaller circle circumference string. The circumference of the outer circle is twice as long.]

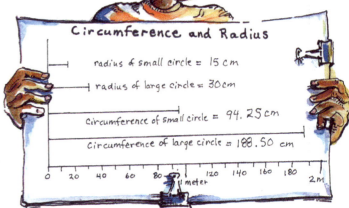

2. Ask who remembers how the radii of the two circles compare? [The larger circle's radius is twice as long as the smaller circle.] To help individuals understand the relationship between the radius and circumference of one circle to another one, show the group the "Circumference and Radius" chart. Ask:
   - ❀ How much longer is the radius of the large circle than the small circle? [twice as long]
   - ❀ How much longer is the circumference of the large circle to the small circle? [twice as long]
   - ❀ How would you describe the relationship between the length of the radius and the length of the circumference? [direct relationship — if the radius of one circle is twice as long as the radius of another circle, the circumference will also be twice as long]
   - ❀ If our circle's radius was five times longer, how much longer would the circumference be of the new circle? [five times as long]

Making Circle-Shaped Beds

Distribute the Radius Measurement Tools, pencils, and 1-meter lengths of string to the teams. Let the youth create their circular planting beds. Oversee them to ensure there is space to walk around each bed and that the beds don't overlap. Remind them to keep the measuring tools taut while drawing the circles.

Planting on Radii and Diameters

1. After the circles are drawn in the soil, have each group lay its 1-meter string across the circles through the center point.

2. Give each group 9 flower seedlings. Have them plant one seedling at the center point and a seedling at each point where the string crosses the circumferences of the circles.

3. Tell them to rotate the string 90° and repeat the step of planting the remaining 4 seedlings.

4. As you visit the teams, check for understanding by having them point out the radii and diameters of their concentric circles.

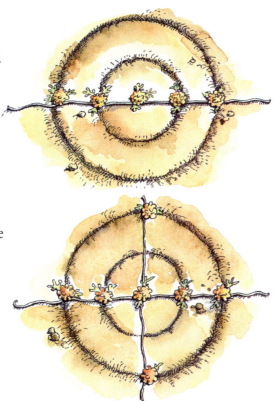

Planting A Salad

1. As teams finish planting their flowers, have them return to you for their seed-packet bundle. Let them decide where they want to plant each crop on their circles. Assist, as needed, with the planting.

2. In their journals, have the youth draw their planting circles showing where they planted the seeds and seedlings, and the distances between the circles and the plants. Tell them to label circumference, diameter, and radius. Also label where they planted each crop.
   Ask:
   ❀ How do the concentric circle garden beds compare to a rainbow?

Seen from an airplane a rainbow forms concentric circles; from the ground, we see part of those circles as concentric arcs.

3. Water the seeds and seedlings before leaving the garden.

More Math in the Garden

Measuring Circles Use various standard unit measuring tools (measuring tape, yardstick, meter stick) to measure the radius, diameter, and circumferences of different circle beds.

MATH IN THE GARDEN

Pattern Snacks

Ages 5-13

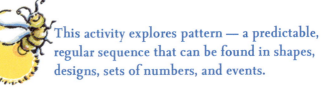

This activity explores pattern — a predictable, regular sequence that can be found in shapes, designs, sets of numbers, and events.

The garden's harvest is filled with myriad shapes and colors that make interesting patterns. Using a variety of fresh fruits and vegetables, youth design patterns and identify "secret" patterns created by members of their group.

What You Need

For Each Person
- paper plate
- paper napkin
- journal
- pencil and crayons

For the Group
- 3 to 5 different foods, at least 20 items per person, for example:
  - **Vegetables** (carrot sticks or rounds, celery sticks, jicama cubes, cauliflowers)
  - **Fruits** (grapes, zucchini rounds, cherry tomatoes, cucumber rounds)
  - **Grains** (whole grain cereal, pretzels)
- knife and cutting board
- serving implements and containers
- databoard
- 3 colors of marking pens

Getting Ready

1. Cut the fresh fruits and vegetables into small rounds, cubes, or sticks, and put each type of food into a separate container with a serving tool.

2. On the databoard, draw a simple pattern to use as an example. You might alternate a carrot stick with two grapes. Repeat the pattern on the paper: carrot, grape, grape, carrot, grape, grape.

110   MATH IN THE GARDEN

Here We Go

1. Gather the group near the picnic table with the plates of food. Display your sketch of the foods arranged in a pattern. Ask the children:
   - What is the next food I should draw to keep this pattern going? [carrot, then grape, then grape]
   - What makes a pattern? [repeating something]
   - Where have you seen patterns? [clothes, floors, jewelry, soccer ball]

It is important to model a complete pattern extended neatly in a line. Young children who are unfamiliar with patterns are inclined to create pictures with the food rather than a repeating pattern.

2. Point out that the "identity" or "secret" of a pattern is the order of the items that make the pattern. Patterns are repetitions. They can involve many things, such as shape, color, and size.

3. Ask how can we convert our food pattern to a letter pattern? [substitute the letter "a" for carrot and the letter "b" for grape: abbabbabb]

Creating a Secret Pattern

1. Show the children the food they will use to make food patterns. Tell them that while creating patterns they will taste and eat fresh plant snacks. With everyone watching, create a food pattern on a napkin spread on the picnic table. Ask them to say the color, shape, and name of each item as you create your pattern. As you complete the second repetition of the pattern, invite youth to suggest which food will be added next.

MATH IN THE GARDEN

2. Tell the group that there are several goals for the activity. You hope that they will taste at least one new food while exploring healthy snacks and creating "secret" patterns. Encourage them to taste something new or something they haven't eaten in some time. Point out that taste preferences change and people often discover they like something they previously disliked.

Research shows that people frequently need to taste something more than 11 times before they include it in their diets.

3. Ask children to suggest ways to share the food fairly and post their guidelines. [take only one or two of the snacks until everyone has made their selection; if you touch it, you must eat it; ask leader before taking seconds]

4. Direct them to create a pattern, record it in their journal, and ask a partner to identify the secret rule using a letter code. Let them snack on extra items while they create and share.

5. As the children work, ask guiding questions to assess their knowledge of patterns:
   ❃ How many different colors and shapes do you plan to use in your pattern?
   ❃ How do you know what comes next in your pattern?

6. Remind them to record their patterns in their journals.

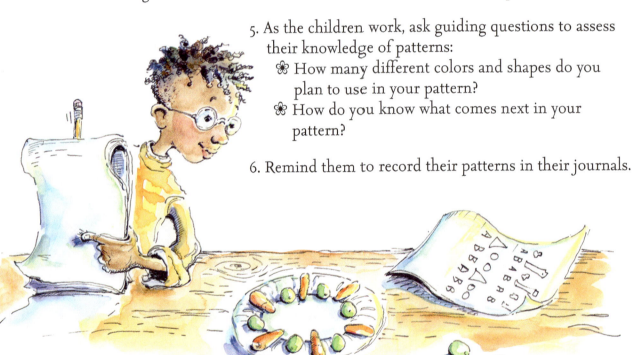

Finding the Secret to a Pattern

1. Have everyone stand for a "Pattern Walk" around the picnic table to view the tasty creations. Encourage the youth to guess silently the "secret patterns" as they progress from pattern to pattern.

2. When all patterns have been viewed, ask the youth to describe the patterns they saw:
    ❀ Which patterns were similar? In what ways?
    ❀ What was the most unusual pattern?
    ❀ Which patterns were difficult to figure out?

3. If a pattern was not identified, ask the designer to reveal the "secret" code.

Older children will sometimes create Fibonacci spirals and complex rotational designs that do not conform to the repetitive rule but are examples of sequences and designs. Thank them for their extra efforts.

4. As everyone eats his or her food pattern, ask:
    ❀ What did you like about creating patterns?
    ❀ How many different ways have you used patterns other than in this activity?
    ❀ How can you teach your family about patterns?
        ❀ What other patterns can you create from different things?

More Math in the Garden

Designing Geometric Snacks Have youth design snacks that display various geometric shapes and examples of symmetry.

Analyzing What We Eat Determine children's preferences for the various snack items by tallying or weighing foods before and after the snack.

Making New Pattern Snacks Repeat this activity again when you have snacks with your group.

Symmetry — Find That Line

Ages 5-8

This activity explores bilateral symmetry and asymmetry.

Children investigate the symmetry of their own bodies, as well as of leaves and other objects from the garden. They also discover objects that are asymmetrical (not symmetrical). Identifying the presence of symmetry in objects allows children to classify different types of regular patterns and distinguish between them. Bilateral symmetry means that the right half of an object is essentially the same as its left half.

What You Need

For Each Pair
- 12-inch piece of string
- rectangular plastic mirror
- journals
- pencils and crayons

For the Group
- 4-foot length of string
- 12-inch length of string
- symmetrical leaf
- asymmetrical leaf
- asymmetrical or symmetrical item from the garden
- databoard
- colored marking pens

Getting Ready

Gather the string and materials and visit the garden to collect symmetrical and asymmetrical leaves and objects.

MATH IN THE GARDEN

Here We Go

1. Ask the children what they know about symmetry.

2. Invite a volunteer to be your model as you hold up a 4-foot length of string that extends head to toe. Position the string in front of the child to create a line of symmetry that evenly divides the head and torso.

3. Ask the other children to look closely on both sides of the string and note what is the "same" on both sides, such as number and size of eyes, nostrils, arms, feet. Tell the children that certain parts of the body have symmetry — there is a matching body part on both sides of the line that divides the body. If you could fold the body in half, both sides closely correspond. A butterfly demonstrates this type of symmetry, too. We call this bilateral symmetry.

> Bilateral symmetry (also called line symmetry and reflectional symmetry) is present in an object when the reflected image in the mirror held along the object's midline looks like the half of the actual object the image replaces.

4. Ask what is different on each side of the child, such as rings or a watch worn on only one side of the body. Tell them we would describe this lack of correspondence in the jewelry as having asymmetry.

5. Place the string across the waist of another child. Ask:
   ❀ Does this line divide the body symmetrically? [no]
      ❀ Why or why not? [the two halves are different]
      ❀ What do we call this lack of symmetry? [asymmetry]

Symmetry in the Garden

1. Hold up the symmetrical leaf from the garden. Ask:
   ❀ Does the leaf look symmetrical?
   ❀ Why or why not? [it can be folded in half and the halves match]

2. Take the leaf and place it on the databoard. Have a child who thinks it is symmetrical place a string along a line of symmetry on the leaf. Ask:
   ❀ Why do you think that it is a line of symmetry? [both sides look almost exactly alike]
   ❀ Are there any other lines of symmetry on this leaf?

3. Fold the leaf in half and show that the two halves are almost identical in shape and size. In the natural world it is unlikely to find perfectly symmetrical objects, however botanists would say that the plant leaf exhibits bilateral symmetry.

4. Open the leaf and place a mirror along the line of symmetry. The reflected image in the mirror looks like the half of the leaf it is covering up. Have them look in the mirror to check that the reflection approximately matches the half of the leaf it is hiding.

Asymmetry in the Garden

1. Hold up the asymmetrical leaf from the garden. Ask:
   ❖ Can this leaf be folded in half so that the two halves fit exactly on top of each other? [no, the two halves do not match in shape or size]

2. Let children try to place the string along a line of symmetry. Identify the parts of the leaf that do not match up.

3. Place the mirror on a possible line of symmetry. Have the children look in the mirror to see what the symmetrical half would look like. Point out the parts that do not match the actual half of the leaf hidden by the mirror.

4. Invite a volunteer to remind the group of the term that is used for objects that have no line of symmetry. [asymmetrical]

5. Show your other item from the garden, such as a brick or hoe. Ask the children to categorize it as being symmetrical or asymmetrical and to explain their reasoning.

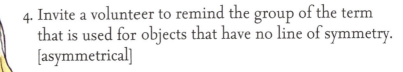

Finding Lines of Symmetry

1. Give each pair of children a mirror and string and challenge them to find and record at least two different symmetrical items in the garden following these steps:

116   MATH IN THE GARDEN

a. Select an object in the garden.
b. If it is small enough, place the mirror on the midline. If the object is too big for the mirror, lay the string along its midline.
c. Use the mirror to compare the reflection to the half of the actual object that is hidden. Use the string to compare the two halves.
d. If the object is symmetrical, draw and label it in your journal.
e. Use the string or mirror on your drawing to make sure there is a line of symmetry.

2. Gather the group and let pairs share the items they found that were symmetrical. You may want to revisit some items to verify the lines of symmetry.

3. Ask:

   ❦ What things in the garden are likely to have a line of symmetry?
   ❦ What things in the garden are not likely to have a line of symmetry?
   ❦ What kind of people use symmetry in their jobs? [architects, artists, dentists]

More Math in the Garden

Symmetry Everywhere Encourage children to look for items that display bilateral symmetry at home, in school, and in the garden. Categorize them as "natural" or human-made.

Dissecting Fruits Have children harvest fruits and vegetables from the garden and cut them open to check for symmetry. The following activity, "Symmetry inside Fruit," explores rotational symmetry.

Impressions of Symmetry Children make rubbings of garden leaves, then check them for symmetry.

Symmetry Inside Fruit

Ages 5-13

This activity explores bilateral symmetry, rotational symmetry, and asymmetry.

Youth harvest and dissect fruits from the garden. Before cutting them open, they compare the shapes and sizes and predict what's inside. Within the fruit they discover beautiful designs and structures, many of which have influenced art and architecture. They prepare delicious snacks from the garden harvest.

What You Need

For Each Pair
- rectangular plastic mirror
- 12-inch piece of string
- journals
- pencils and crayons

For the Group
- selection of fruits, at least 2 of each kind
- cutting board
- knife
- flagging, such as ribbon or plastic tape
- 12-inch piece of string

MATH IN THE GARDEN

Getting Ready

1. Check the garden for fruits that are ready for harvest, and flag those plants that may be picked by the children. If the ripe produce is meager, purchase some items from the store to provide greater variety. Be sure there are at least two of each fruit for each person, including yourself, because one of each fruit will be cut vertically and the other horizontally. For your demonstration, try to use fruit that is different from what youth will be examining so you do not steal their surprise.

2. Gather the mirrors, string, and materials needed to harvest, clean, and prepare the fruits for observation and tasting. Depending on the age of your children, you may want to allow them to use plastic knives to dissect thin-skinned fruits. For fruit with tough outer coverings, like gourds and melons, create a "dissection station" where you will use a sharp knife to make the cuts.

Here We Go

1. Gather the group in the garden, and tell them that they get to harvest fruits from the plants that you have flagged. If they don't already know the botanical definition of "fruit," explain that a fruit is the part of the plant that contains seeds. Cucumbers, tomatoes, and bell peppers are fruits that are commonly called "vegetables," which is a term used in cooking.

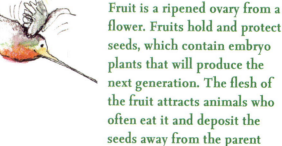

Fruit is a ripened ovary from a flower. Fruits hold and protect seeds, which contain embryo plants that will produce the next generation. The flesh of the fruit attracts animals who often eat it and deposit the seeds away from the parent plant. This helps move plants from one place to another.

2. Ask each pair to choose a different fruit to harvest. Have them pick two of their fruits, and bring the produce back to the group area. As pairs return, have them place their harvested items on a picnic table or surface that can be viewed easily

by everyone. Pick two fruits yourself to use in your demonstration.

3. Select one of your fruits and ask children to observe it from different perspectives and describe the attributes of shape, size, color, texture, and smell.

4. Tell them you are going to cut the fruit in half. What do they think it will look like inside? Encourage them to give rich descriptions that connect to past experiences with similar fruits.

What's Inside the Fruit?

1. Place the fruit on the cutting board and explain that you will use the science method of "dissection" to cut it in half bilaterally so that both halves are almost identical. Have youth observe the two halves and encourage them to look for patterns. Ask questions such as:
   ❀ What do you see inside?
   ❀ How does the design on one half compare to the one on the other half?
   ❀ How can we determine if a design is symmetrical?

2. Show them how to position a string across the center of the cut surface on one half of the fruit to check for symmetry on both sides of the string. Have them also place a mirror along the line of symmetry. The reflected image in the mirror looks like the half of the fruit it is covering up. Have them look in the mirror to check that the reflection approximately matches the half of the cut surface it is hiding.

3. If the interior of the cut does not have symmetry, explain that the term we use is "asymmetry."

4. Take a second piece of the same fruit you just cut open. How does the shape and size of this whole fruit compare to the one just cut?

5. Tell children that this time you are going to cut the fruit in half along a midline perpendicular to the first cut. Demonstrate where you plan to make the cut. Ask them to predict what the fruit will look like inside after this cut.

6. Cut the fruit in half and show the insides of the two halves. Ask:
   ❀ How does the internal design of this cut compare to the design revealed by the other cut?

7. Have them look carefully at the halves and check for symmetry. If this cut reveals rotational symmetry as depicted in the illustration of the green apple (page 120), draw their attention to the way the internal pattern in the fruit is repeated around a central point.

> Rotational symmetry is present when a shape is repeated around a fixed point.

Dissecting and Observing Fruit

1. Tell partners they will have a chance to dissect a fruit to see what's inside. If you plan to have them use plastic knives, review knife safety.

2. Explain the steps they will follow:
   a. Draw a picture of the fruit and label it.
   b. Agree which direction to cut it in half at a midline.
   c. Predict what it will look like inside.
   d. Cut it open. Describe the inside.
   e. Check for symmetry (bilateral, rotational, asymmetry).
   f. Use a string or mirror to assist.
   g. Draw the inside design of the fruit.
   h. Cut the second fruit perpendicular to the first cut and repeat these steps.

> Depending on the age of your children, you may want to guide the group through the steps with a second fruit example, predicting, cutting, and observing a vertical cut followed by a horizontal cut.

3. Have pairs select two fruits of the same kind to cut and observe. Have them draw and label their designs in their journals. Invite those who finish early to harvest and investigate a second kind of fruit.

4. Gather as a group. Have youth share their findings. Sort the fruit halves so that ones with similar designs inside are grouped.
   ❊ How many fruits had lines of symmetry?
   ❊ What kinds of symmetry did you find? Rotational symmetry? Bilateral symmetry? Asymmetry?

5. While you and the group enjoy fruit snacks from the garden, encourage everyone to continue their explorations at home with other fruits and vegetables and share what they observe with their families.

More Math in the Garden

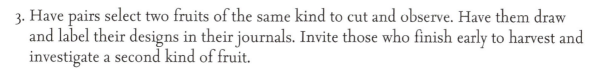

Cutting on the Diagonal Have children make diagonal cuts in fruits and vegetables. What patterns and designs emerge with this type of slice?

Printing with Symmetry Cut fruits and vegetables to make natural block prints. Have children create print designs that are symmetrical.

Drawing Tree Observations

Ages 5-8

Children sketch a tree in the garden. They then observe patterns of leaves, symmetry and asymmetry, angles of branching, and shapes of foliage. They make a second sketch of the tree, applying their recent experiences observing the natural geometry of plants. During a "Tree Art Gallery," the individuals compare their own "before" and "after" drawings, noting similarities and differences.

This activity develops skills of estimating proportions, identifying shapes and patterns, and drawing to scale.

What You Need

For Each Person
- 2 to 4 sheets of paper
- pencil
- crayons or colored pencils

Getting Ready

1. Pick a tree in the garden for the children to draw.

2. Assemble drawing materials and journals.

MATH IN THE GARDEN

Here We Go

1. Gather the children about 20 feet away from a tree to give everyone enough room to draw. Have them draw the tree, and put their name and date on the drawing.

2. When the children finish, collect the drawings. Tell them they will be discussing the drawings later in the actiity.

Discovering Geometry in Trees

1. Explain that the group will start by observing the tree to see if it is symmetrical, or the same on both halves. To do this, have children close one eye, hold their pencil upright, and line it up with the tree trunk.
   Guide their observation of the tree and ask:
   ❁ What things are the same on both sides of the tree?
   ❁ What things are different?
   ❁ How many big branches are on each side?
   ❁ Which side has the most leaves?

2. Have them open both eyes and observe the tree's canopy. Ask:
   ❁ About how far up from the ground do the branches start?
   ❁ How do the branches grow out from the trunk? Do they reach up, grow straight out, or droop toward the ground?
   ❁ How do the shapes and sizes of the leaves vary?
   ❁ How are the leaves positioned on the tree?

3. Move the children close to the tree trunk and look up.
   ❁ How do the branches grow? Do they circle the trunk in a spiral or grow mostly on one side or the other?

MATH IN THE GARDEN

- ❀ How do the smaller branches grow from the larger branches?
- ❀ Is there a pattern in the way they grow?

4. Encourage them to use math language to describe details of the tree.
   - ❀ How many holes do you see in the trunk and branches?
   - ❀ Where do you see triangles in the tree?
   - ❀ How many leaves fit in your hand span?

Drawing Again and Comparing

1. Have children draw the tree again, this time adding details from their closer observation, such as tree structures, angles, shapes, and patterns. Give the children adequate time to draw.

2. Invite those who finish early to select and draw a different tree or plant.

3. Gather the group in a circle and redistribute the first drawings. Have children stand in a circle and display their two drawings by holding them side-by-side to make a "Tree Art Gallery." Ask everyone silently to view the gallery drawings. Tell them that each child will be asked to compare his or her own drawings. To guide their comparisons, ask:
   - ❀ What are some things that are the same in your two drawings?
   - ❀ How are the branches different in the two drawings?
   - ❀ Which tree drawing has more leaves?
   - ❀ What patterns did you observe?
   - ❀ How did you use math in your drawing?

In this review of art, children report on their own drawings and do not critique the work of others.

4. Thank everyone for their contributions to the "Tree Art Gallery" and ask a few reflective questions in closing.
    - ❀ If you were to draw the tree a third time, what changes might you make?
    - ❀ What kinds of jobs use drawing skills?
      [carpenter, electrician, inventor, landscape architect, biologist, fashion designer]

More Math in the Garden

Documenting Changes in the Garden Conduct drawing sessions throughout the seasons. Encourage children to look for numbers, shapes, symmetry, perspectives, bilateral symmetry, and patterns in the growing plants.

"Symmetry — Find that Line!" is a helpful activity either to precede or follow this one, because it explores reflectional symmetry and asymmetry in the garden.

MATH IN THE GARDEN

CHAPTER FOUR
Data Analysis

The garden provides an exciting arena in which to collect, organize, and analyze information. Children's thinking and reasoning skills are developed and honed as they create tables and graphs and compare the data they collect for flowers, shadows, and plant predators. Data can be displayed in many different ways to give us information, and the way the data is organized influences our interpretation. Being able to analyze the data critically to determine the "facts" versus the "inferences" allows us to make informed decisions.

Data is often collected using tally marks, and then the number of occurrences is counted and recorded. Tables and graphs are the two common methods of displaying data. Frequency tables show how often something occurs. Graphs create a visual representation of the data, and include bar graphs, pictographs, circle graphs, and line graphs.

Data analysis includes statistics. Common statistics related to collection of data are the "average" or mean, the mode (most frequently occurring number), and the median (the value that falls in the middle of a distribution, above and below which lie an equal number of values). These are all measures of central tendency.

The activities in this chapter provide engaging opportunities to identify attributes of data, determine frequency, create graphs, and interpret data. In particular, the "Flowers: Graph and Graph Again" activity provides an opportunity for children to see how the same data can be displayed in two distinct graphs and provide very different information.

Data Snacks

Ages 5-13

This activity introduces data collection and interpretation, including the meaning of range.

Youth explore a variety of fresh fruit and vegetable snacks and analyze their food preferences. They predict which food will be eaten by the greatest number of people in the group and compute the actual results. This activity models methods that children can use in many areas of their lives to investigate questions that interest them.

What You Need

For Each Person
- paper plate
- napkin
- journal
- pencil

For the Group
- 4 to 5 different kinds of fresh plant snacks in about equal quantities, such as carrots, celery sticks, zucchini rounds, grapes, cucumber slices, olives, popcorn, and cherry tomatoes
- knife
- cutting board
- serving implements and containers
- paper towels
- databoard
  – "Snack Data" chart
  – paper for data collection ideas
- colored marking pen
- several pieces of paper to make "tent" labels

MATH IN THE GARDEN

Getting Ready

1. Gather and prepare the food items to exhibit a variety of fruits and vegetables from the garden. Place each type of food in its own container.

2. On the picnic table, arrange the containers of food in a line that can be easily viewed by the group and sampled in a buffet style. To make sure that favorite foods are not taken before everyone gets a chance to sample, distribute them evenly along the line.

3. Cut the paper into strips and make "tent" labels for each snack item.

4. On the databoard, make a "Snack Data" chart listing the foods to be sampled.

Here We Go

1. Gather the group around a picnic table and show them the snack buffet and the "Snack Data" chart. Ask the youth to silently think about which of the various foods they have tasted. They can share this information later.

2. Tell them you want to find out more about what they like to eat and to let them taste some new foods. Explain that a goal of the snack experience is to increase the variety of fresh fruits and vegetables they have eaten.

3. Ask the youth to predict silently which food item they think will be eaten by the greatest number of people in the group.

4. Ask:
   - What are some ways we can find out what snack will be eaten by the most people? List their ideas on the databoard and help them formulate data collection methods. [counting how many tried each snack; having each person record how many of each snack he or she ate; having people write their names on a card next to each snack as they take it]

5. Tell them that today we are going to collect data by tally marks. In their journals they should tally the numbers for each item they eat. (If they eat 5 pieces of cucumber they will have 5 tally marks next to cucumber.)

6. Have the children suggest how they will share the food fairly, and post their guidelines. [take only one or two of the snacks until everyone has made their selection; if you touch a piece of food, you must eat it; ask the leader before taking seconds]

Counting, Eating, and Analyzing

1. Observe how the youth make their choices and what they talk about. Encourage them to taste something new or something they haven't eaten in a while. To help you assess their prior experience and stimulate discussion, ask:
   - What new food did you try?
   - How were you surprised by the taste of any of the snacks?
   - What food would you recommend to a friend?
   - Which food did you eat the largest quantity of?
   - Which food did you eat the smallest quantity of?

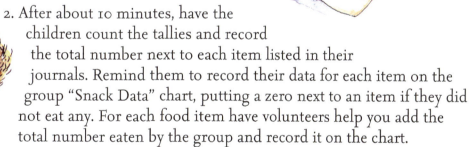

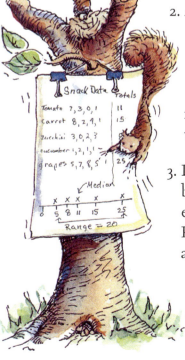

2. After about 10 minutes, have the children count the tallies and record the total number next to each item listed in their journals. Remind them to record their data for each item on the group "Snack Data" chart, putting a zero next to an item if they did not eat any. For each food item have volunteers help you add the total number eaten by the group and record it on the chart.

3. Draw a line near the bottom of the "Snack Data" chart. This will become a numberline for plotting data. Put a "0" at the left-most end of the line, and put the highest total near the right-most end. Place the other totals along the number line with reasonable spacing according to their relative amount.

4. Plot the totals on the numberline. Have volunteers help analyze the data. Ask:
   - What is the largest number to plot on our numberline?

✿ What is the smallest number to plot on our numberline?

5. Point out that the difference between the high and low numbers for the different foods is the range of data for food eaten by our group. [most-often eaten item and least-often eaten item] Invite volunteers to help you identify and record the range of data for the food consumed.

Range = difference between the largest number and smallest number in a data sample. (For example: The range of 25 grapes eaten and 5 cucumbers eaten is 20.)

6. Continue plotting totals until all of the numbers have been plotted on the numberline. Ask:
    ✿ What is the range of the data? [25−5=20]
    ✿ How can we tell which item was tasted by the greatest number of people? [The food item that has the fewest zeros entered for it on the "Snack Data" chart.]

7. Encourage youth to discuss the activity. Ask:
    ✿ What did you like about collecting data on snacks?
    ✿ How could you improve the data-collecting methods for the next time?
    ✿ What helped you decide to try a new food?
    ✿ What did you learn from the "Data Snacks" activity?

More Math in the Garden

Snack Preference Study Each time you have a snack, conduct another snack preference study. Older youth can total the data, compute final averages and percents, and graph results.

Geometric Snacks Have youth design snacks that display various geometric shapes and examples of symmetry.

Leaf Attributes

Ages 5-13

This activity reinforces skills of observation, comparing, matching, and identifying attributes, which are essential to sorting, classifying, and analyzing data.

Youth compare the attributes of various leaves and organize them into an "attribute train" based on shared characteristics. They take a first look at the diversity of plants as expressed through their rich array of leaf form, structure, color, and texture.

What You Need

For Each Person
- journal
- pencil

For the Group
- collection of leaves
- databoards
- transparent tape

MATH IN THE GARDEN

131

Getting Ready

Check on the availability of a variety of leaves in the garden for youth to collect. If leaves are not available, purchase a wide variety of edible leaves for youth to use.

Here We Go

1. Have your group form a circle around you. Pick several individuals who have something visible in common (such as hair, a color of shirt, shoes) to stand in the middle of the circle. Have other children try to guess the common attribute (characteristic). Once it's been guessed, the volunteers leave the center. Select new people with a different attribute to be in the center of the circle for a second round.

2. Invite the youth to gaze around at the amazing variety of garden plants. Explain that the various characteristics of plants help them survive. Tell the youth they will be going on a "Leaf Hunt" in the garden to discover some of these attributes.

Point out that plants form the base of the food pyramid that supports all life on earth. Over millions of years, plants have become adapted to survive challenging environmental factors, such as extremes of weather, plant eaters, and competition for light.

3. To sharpen everyone's leaf observation skills for the hunt, show them the pictures of leaves on the preceding page. Ask questions such as:
   - Which leaves are shaped like your hand? Which are long and thin?
   - Which leaves have edges that are jagged (toothed), smooth, or wavy?
   - Which leaves grow opposite each other on the stem, and which leaves grow in groups of three?

4. Tell the youth they are to look closely at leaves on at least three different plants. Encourage them to compare the features on the different leaves and how they grow from the stem.

5. Have each person bring back one leaf to compare. Caution them to carefully remove the leaf from a low, inconspicuous part of the plant, or better yet, pick it up from the ground.

6. As they observe their leaves, encourage the youth to focus on attributes such as: size, shape, edges, texture, and color. Ask them to remember how the leaf was growing on the plant.

MATH IN THE GARDEN

Comparing Leaves

1. Have the youth compare the similarities and differences among their leaves. Guide them as needed using the illustration on page 131.
   ❀ What type of edge does each leaf have?
   ❀ How many of the leaves have lobed edges?
   ❀ Which has the darkest green color?
   ❀ How are the textures of the leaves similar and different?
   ❀ How many of the leaves are edible?

2. Have the youth sort the leaves into groups. Start with a size sort.
   ❀ Which leaf is the biggest?
   ❀ Which leaf is the smallest?
   ❀ Which leaf size was most common?
   ❀ Which leaf size was the least common?

3. Sort the leaves in other ways. Have the youth suggest other visible common characteristics. Guide them as needed. With each sorting, focus on one major attribute:
   ❀ Green/not green (or by specific colors)
   ❀ Type of edges on the leaf (smooth, serrated, wavy)
   ❀ Texture of the leaf (smooth, prickly, rough)
   ❀ Number of points on the leaf (0, 1, 2, 3 …)

All Aboard the Attribute Train

1. Have the youth create an attribute train with their leaves by placing one leaf after another in a line, based on matching characteristics.

2. Have one person start by taping her leaf to the databoard. Ask her to describe it in as many ways as possible. She might say, "It is little and its edges are smooth. It is shaped like a triangle. It has small vein patterns."

3. Ask if someone has a leaf that matches any one of those characteristics. One child may have another leaf that is little. This one can join the leaf attribute train, since the attribute of size connects the two leaves.

MATH IN THE GARDEN

4. Have this child identify the connecting attribute of size as he tapes it next to the first leaf. Then have him describe several other attributes about his little leaf. He might say, "It has edges like a saw, feels fuzzy, and is dark green on top and whitish underneath."

5. If someone gets stuck trying to find an attribute, have the individual describe the leaves until a common characteristic is revealed.

6. Continue until everyone in the group has placed at least one leaf in the train. You may need to use a second databoard.

7. Go back to the beginning of the train and check to see if children can describe the connections between the leaves. If they have forgotten the original attribute, they can suggest another observable characteristic that leaves next to each other share.

Reflecting on Leaves

1. When you finish with the attribute train, have the youth retrieve their special leaves and tape them in their journals. Ask them to write down (or dictate for you to write down) as many attributes about their leaf as they can.

2. Ask them to write their ideas for how certain attributes might help their plant to capture sunlight and make food, and avoid being eaten by animals. [strong smells deter plant eaters, waxy coating conserves moisture, dark green increases light absorption]

More Math in the Garden

Making Venn Diagrams Make a leaf Venn diagram. Gather a new group of leaves, or use the students' leaves before they tape them into their journals.

1. Have two volunteers place two very different leaves on the databoard, with a space between. Make a circle of string around each leaf.

2. Let the students describe a different main characteristic that distinguishes each leaf and write that description below each leaf.

3. Have the youth sort their remaining leaves into one of the two circles. If a leaf has characteristics of both circles, make the string circles overlap and put that leaf into the overlap.

Comparing Edible Leaves Repeat this activity using leaves such as spinach, lettuce, beets, kale, and cabbage. Youth can also sort leaves they enjoy eating by leaf attributes.

Flowers: Graph & Graph Again

Ages 5-13

This activity introduces basic statistical skills — recording, organizing, and evaluating data.

Children observe a beautiful array of flowers and graph the flowers according to various attributes. The group compares the graphs to see how the same data set can give very different information, depending on how it is organized.

What You Need

For Each Person
- 2 flowers of the same kind
- journal
- pencil and crayons

For the Group
- transparent tape
- large paper plate
- mixed bouquet of flowers
- 3 databoards
  – "Attributes" list
  – "Attribute Categories" chart
  – several sheets of paper
- colored marking pens

Getting Ready

Locate an area of the garden with a wide variety of blossoms, or provide a generous mixed bouquet of flowers from which each youth can select two flowers of the same kind for graphing and a third for the Attribute Train. Try to have a mix of at least 10 different kinds of flowers available that vary in size, colors, and structure.

MATH IN THE GARDEN

Here We Go

1. In the garden have the children look around them and describe what they notice about flowers. What colors are they? How big are they?

This activity is difficult to do if it is at all windy outside. If you collect flowers in advance, this activity can be done in a sheltered space or room.

2. Show the group the flowers they will use in this activity. Let them closely observe several different kinds of flowers. Then have each person carefully choose two flowers of the same kind. Ask everyone to keep one flower and place the other flower on the paper plate for use later in the activity.

3. Distribute journals and crayons, and have each person carefully observe his or her flower and draw it.

4. While the youth are making their drawings, ask observation questions and talk about the flower's attributes (size, shape, edges, color, and how the flower grows on the plant). Encourage them to write three observable characteristics of their flowers next to their drawings.

5. As they finish their drawings, have the youth pair up and compare their flowers. They should find at least two things that are the same and two things that are different about their flowers.

Flowers on a Graph

1. Ask the children to describe one special attribute of their flowers while you list it on the databoard titled "Attributes." Their descriptions are often quite detailed, such as "pale pink and lavender petals." Accept their observations, and if they need to be shortened slightly, check with the child to make certain you have captured the nature of the observation.

2. Title a second databoard, "Attribute Categories" and referring back to the list, have volunteers help you organize the descriptions into "major attributes" (main groups) such as size, color, number of petals, and "subgroups of the attributes" such as size — big, medium, small; color — red, yellow, blue, white; number of petals — 3, 4, 5, more than 10. This is the chart the group will refer to during the graphing activities. See illustration.

136   MATH IN THE GARDEN

3. Place the first databoard, with a clean piece of paper on it, on a picnic table or on the ground. Have youth place their flowers on the databoard.

4. Invite a volunteer to suggest a major attribute, such as number of petals, and write this at the top of the databoard. Ask volunteers to sort the flowers into groups by number of petals.

5. Draw a line near the bottom of the databoard, leaving a little space to label the colors. Assist the group to graph the flowers into columns by petal color.

6. When the graph is complete, have the youth make true statements about the flowers. Assist by asking:
   ❁ How many flowers have 4 petals? (choose an example from your graph)
   ❁ How many more 5-petal flowers than 4-petal flowers are there?
   ❁ How many flowers are there altogether?
   ❁ What is the most common number of petals per flower in our collection?
   ❁ What is a good title for this graph?

7. Tape the organized flowers to the paper so that youth can compare this graph with other graphs that are created later.

Graphing Again

1. Make a second graph next to the first one, using the third databoard and the second flower each student placed on the plate. Using another attribute, such as size, have them sort and graph the flowers in a different way. You will see how data organized differently impacts how it is interpreted.

2. Again, encourage youth to make true statements about a size graph, such as:
   ❁ Which group has the most flowers?
   ❁ How many flowers are medium in size?
   ❁ What other observations can you make about this graph of flowers?
   ❁ How many flowers are there altogether?
   ❁ From this graph can we say there are always fewer large (or small) flowers? [No, this statement is true for this collection of flowers, but another collection of flowers could look completely different.]

3. Ask the group to compare the two graphs:
    ❀ What is the same about each graph?
    ❀ What does each graph tell us about our flowers?
    ❀ Who might be interested in the results of these graphs?

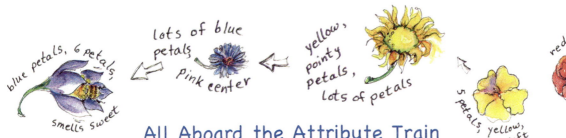

All Aboard the Attribute Train

1. Create an attribute train. Have each child select a new flower. Have one child place a flower on a new data sheet, and describe as many visible attributes as possible. He may say, "It's red. It has five petals shaped like feathers. All the petals look the same."

2. Ask if someone has a flower that matches one of those attributes. For example, someone may have a red flower that can become part of the train. The attribute of red color connects the two flowers.

3. Have this child identify the connecting attribute of red color as she tapes it next to the first flower. Then have her describe several other attributes about her flower. She may say, "The petals are big and small. There are yellow hairs in the middle, and there are many, many petals."

4. Continue until all the youth have placed one flower after another in the train and described the connecting attribute.

5. If you have time, return to the first flower and see if the children can remember the observable characteristic that flowers next to each other share.

More Math in the Garden

More Graphing Provide children with edible leaves or nuts and seeds to graph in a similar way.

Abstract Graphs Have older youths make abstract graphs based on the flower graphs already made. See examples at right.

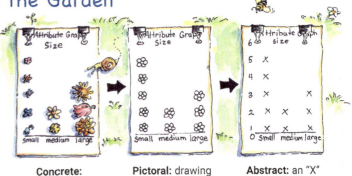

Concrete: actual flower

Pictoral: drawing represents a flower

Abstract: an "X" represents a flower

138   MATH IN THE GARDEN

What's in Garden Soil?

Ages 5-13

This activity explores classifying and analyzing data.

Youth examine a sample of garden soil and sort the various components to discover the amazing variety of items that make up the soil mixture. They classify ingredients into two major categories: organic and inorganic. Then they sort each category further into groups such as rocks, pebbles, and sand. A major goal of the activity is to spark their curiosity about the wonders of natural soil.

What You Need

For Each Person
- 2 flat toothpicks
- cardboard and paper, 11" x 17"
- journal
- pencil and crayons

For the Group
- several plastic spoons of the same size
- 3 to 4 labeled containers of dry garden soil
- 2 databoards and sketch
   – "What's in Soil?" chart
   – "Organic/Inorganic" chart
   – sketch of sorting circles
- marking pens
- several magnifiers

Getting Ready

1. This activity is most successful when conducted on a calm day with children working at benches or picnic tables. Collect garden soil samples from several areas that haven't been watered recently. Dry garden soil is easier to sort and contains fewer soil organisms.

2. Gather several magnifiers for youth to share to observe the small details of the soil. You will need to carefully supervise the use of these. Most youth are tempted by the opportunity to focus light on tinder to create fire.

3. Make a chart entitled "What's in Soil?" for one databoard (see illustration below). On the other databoard mark a black line dividing the chart in half vertically. Title the left side of the chart "Organic" with a bright-colored pen. Use a different bright color to write "Inorganic" on the right side of the chart (see art page 142). On a new piece of paper, draw and label two large sorting circles, "Organic" and "Inorganic." Clip this underneath the "Organic/Inorganic" chart (see art page 141).

4. Gather 11" x 17" cardboard and paper for youth to use as sorting platforms for their soil samples.

This is a difficult activity to do in the garden if the weather is windy or rainy. If you collect garden soil samples in advance, the activity can be done in a sheltered space or room.

Here We Go

1. Ask the group why they think soil is important. [plants grow in it, food crops need soil, animals live in it] Point out that soil is a mixture of many different things, some of which traveled many miles before ending up in the garden.

2. Invite them to predict items they will find in a spoonful of the garden soil and list these on the "What's in Soil?" chart. This list will give everyone ideas about the things they might find in their own samples, so prompt them to remember what they have seen on the soil surface in the garden.

3. Tell them gardeners sometimes talk about the "organic" and "inorganic" components of soil because a fertile soil needs both. Display the "Organic/Inorganic" chart, with its titles written in bright colors. "Organic" is a term used for ingredients that are alive or were alive in the past. Ask volunteers to help you identify some of the organic items listed on the "What's in Soil?" chart. As youth suggest an item, check or underline it in the same bright color. [leaves, bark, roots, sticks, insects, seed, mushrooms] Point out that organic matter helps soil stay moist and provides nutrients important for plant growth.

4. Explain that soil also contains particles that have worn off rocks and mountains and tumbled through storms and streams. These items, which have never been alive, are termed "inorganic" and provide minerals that are important for plant growth. Have the group help you identify and color-code the inorganic items on the "What's in Soil?" chart. [sand, pebbles, clay, dirt, dust, rocks, silt]

5. Review the "What's in Soil?" chart, checking that the color codes are correct and discussing items that raise questions. For example, youth may want to create an "other" category for human-made objects such as trash.

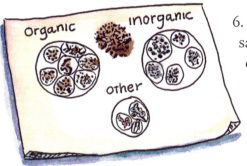

6. Explain that everyone will study a small soil sample, sorting the various items into these two major categories: organic and inorganic. Display your sorting circles illustration, and tell them that they will make two big circles like the ones shown, and label one "Organic" and the other "Inorganic." With the group gathered round, demonstrate how to place a spoonful of soil between the two circles. Continue by showing the children how to use the toothpicks to drag an item, such as a leaf, over to the "Organic" circle. Ask for a volunteer to drag an inorganic item, such as a pebble, to the "Inorganic" circle.

7. Demonstrate how to group items as they are dragged into the big circles. All the bits of leaves get pulled to one area, the twigs to another. Likewise they should make subgroups for the sand, rocks, and silt. If there is an item that they are unsure of, or which doesn't occur naturally in the garden, such as trash, tell them to draw a third circle and label it "Other."

Sorting Soil Ingredients

1. Distribute the equipment and direct everyone to collect their soil samples and begin sorting. Distribute magnifiers to those who would like to look more closely at their soil. As you circulate among the children, encourage them to tell you why they have sorted an item into the "Organic" or "Inorganic" category, and to describe their smaller groupings within the circles.

2. Ask how their soil samples compare with the group's predictions. Have they found examples of all the things listed under "What's in Soil?" What new kinds of items did they find? Were there items that didn't fit in either the "Organic" or "Inorganic" category? [toys, trash]

3. Remind them to draw lines around the subgroups within the categories "Organic" and "Inorganic" so that similar components, such as pieces of bark, are separated from leaves, seeds, and twigs. Direct them to label each subgroup.

If you find critters, point out that most soil organisms are desirable and harmless. Encourage children to gently collect the organisms in a "bug box" to share with the group, and to release in the garden at a later time.

4. How many subgroups did they find in the "Organic" category? Write the number in their journals next to that heading. How many subgroups did they find in the "Inorganic" category? Write the number in their journals next to that heading.

5. When youth have completed their sorting and recorded the subgroups in their journals, call them together to share their findings.

Analyzing the Data

1. Display the "Organic/Inorganic" chart. Ask a volunteer to share one subgroup she found and how she classified it: "Organic" or "Inorganic." Write it in the appropriate column. Now ask for a show of hands of those who also found this material in their sample. Record this number next to the name of the subgroup.

2. Continue to survey the group, writing down the subgroups under "Organic" or "Inorganic," and recording the count of individuals who found the materials in samples. When all the findings have been recorded, guide the group in discussing the findings:
   - What "Organic" subgroup is reported most often? How many people report they find this in their soil sample?
   - What "Organic" subgroup is reported least often? How many people report finding this in their sample?

3. Point out that the difference between the high and low number in the organic category represents the range of data for presence of soil components in the samples. [most often reported item minus least often reported item]

142　　MATH IN THE GARDEN

4. Invite volunteers to help you identify and record the range of data for the "Inorganic" category of soil. Ask:
   - What "Inorganic" subgroup is reported most often? How many people report they find this in their soil sample?
   - What is the least-often reported "Inorganic" subgroup? How many people report finding this in their sample?
   - Which category, "Organic" or "Inorganic," had the most subgroups within it? [Depending on the soil type, rich garden soil will often have more different subgroups of organic material.]
   - Why do you think finding the ranges for soil components can be helpful for a gardener? [help identify garden areas with poor soil or especially rich soil]
   - Which component do you think is greater in our garden soil, the organic material or the inorganic material? Why?
   - What other methods could we use to measure and compare the organic and inorganic materials?

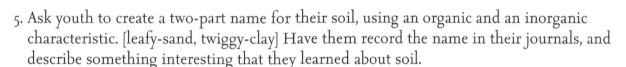

5. Ask youth to create a two-part name for their soil, using an organic and an inorganic characteristic. [leafy-sand, twiggy-clay] Have them record the name in their journals, and describe something interesting that they learned about soil.

More Math in the Garden

Comparing Soils Have children compare the ingredients of a commercial soil mix to natural garden soil. "Soil + Water Profile" on page 47 is an excellent activity to conduct after dry soil has been observed.

Making Seed Balls Autumn is a good time to make native wildflower seed balls. Mix seeds with compost, water, and a little clay, and work the sticky mixture into balls the size of small plums. Dry the seed balls overnight, and toss along roadsides to await the winter rains and the warmth of spring.

Garden Soil Art Soil rubbings and soil collages are fun ways to document characteristics of the garden soil. Don't forget to sense and enjoy the rich soil of the garden.

Plant Predators — Sampling Evidence

Ages 5-13

This activity provides the opportunity to collect, record, organize, and evaluate data.

Youth use a simple sampling technique to gather evidence of plant predators in the garden. They record and organize data from the sampling to determine if there is a problem with animals that are eating the vegetation in the garden.

What You Need

For Each Pair
- leaves with munch holes or slime trails
- leaves with damage due to weather
- red crayon, blue crayon
- 10 wooden craft sticks
- 3 to 4 meters of string
- journals
- pencils

For the Group
- 2 databoards
  - "Sampling Steps" chart
  - "Damage in the Garden" chart
- colored marking pens
- extra wooden craft sticks

Getting Ready

1. Visit the garden to lay out a sample plot for your demonstration. Use a string to encircle 10 of the same kind of plants, some of which exhibit animal damage. You will need to lay out all the plots for young children. Youth 8 years and older will be able to select their own areas and lay out their own plots.

2. Prepare the needed charts for the databoards. For "Sampling Steps" copy steps 1-7 on page 146. For "Damage in the Garden," see illustration on page 147.

144   MATH IN THE GARDEN

3. Collect examples of leaves that have been damaged by animals and weather.

4. When children find plant predators, the animals often steal the show. Follow the steps in "What if You Find Plant Predators?" (page 146) to take advantage of this teachable moment. It may be best to direct the youth's energy and excitement into exploring plant predators and return to assessing damage in plants on another day, when the group will approach collecting damage data with new interest.

Here We Go

1. Ask the youth if anyone has noticed leaves with chew marks. Distribute several kinds of damaged leaves so that each person has an example, and ask volunteers to describe what they see:
   * What kinds of damage do you see?
   * What might be causing this damage? [insects, snails, sun, wind]
   * About how much of your leaf is damaged? [more than half, a little]
   * Who has damage they think was caused by some kind of animal?
   * What clues indicate an animal was eating the leaf? [holes in the middle of the leaf, wandering paths, clusters of scale, small galls]
   * Who has damage they think was caused by the weather?
   * What clues suggest damage by weather? [wind tears at the edges of leaves, sunburn, frostbite]

2. Announce that the group will help find out if the garden has a pest problem. Explain that it would be very difficult to examine every plant in the garden. The youth will work in pairs to examine some small samples of plants from several areas of the garden. This sample system will help them estimate the general level of damage that is occurring.

Demonstrating Data Sampling

1. Gather the group around your sample plot, and ask them to count the number of plants you have enclosed with the string.

2. Ask them what advantages there might be to sampling 10 of the same kind of plants. [10 is a manageable number to examine, not too big or too small. If all the teams are examining a sample of 10, the data can be compared more easily.]

3. Point out that you chose 10 for convenience in this first study, but that scientists often use very complex sampling methods to insure that a study is conducted in a fair way.

Here We Go

Show the "Sampling Steps" chart outlining steps 1-7 below, and ask a volunteer to help you demonstrate the steps that everyone will use to rate the presence or absence of damage. Children will work in pairs.

1. In your journals write the name of the plant you will sample and the date. Make a "No Damage" or "Some Damage" chart.
2. With string, encircle 10 of the same kind of plant in your plot.
3. Check one of the 10 plants in your sample plot for damage.
4. If there is no damage, color the top of a craft stick BLUE on both sides and place it upright in the ground next to the plant.
5. If there is some damage, color the top of a craft stick RED on both sides and place it upright in the ground next to the plant.
6. Tally the damage on your "No Damage" or "Some Damage" chart in your journals.
7. Examine all 10 plants, then total and record the tallies. Record your data on the group chart.

Collecting the Data

1. Distribute the materials and send the pairs off to begin their investigations. Circulate among them, checking that partners have enclosed 10 sample plants with the string.

What if You Find Plant Predators?

1. If youth find a plant predator, use the opportunity to make it the focus of other observations. Ask:
    - What part of the plant is it eating?
    - How much of the leaf has been eaten?
    - Do any other leaves have similar damage?
    - How many plant predators do you think are affecting the plants?

2. Point out that some plant predators are desirable. Butterfly gardens provide food for caterpillars and nectar for butterflies. Discuss when a plant predator is desirable and when it is undesirable.

3. Children can collect suspected plant predators in a clear container to share with others. If the predator is desirable, such as a native butterfly caterpillar, return it to the garden.

MATH IN THE GARDEN

2. Check that the children are examining each plant in their sample plot for evidence of predators. As each plant is checked, have them place one craft stick — colored blue for "No Damage" or red for "Some Damage" — upright in the ground next to the plant.

3. Remind them to record the tally for each plant in their journals.

4. When all the plants in the sample plot have been examined and labeled, have pairs add up the tallies for "No Damage" and "Some Damage" and enter their results on the "Damage in the Garden" chart.

Discussing the Data

1. Ask questions about the results of the samplings of the garden plants:
    - Which kind of plant had the least evidence of damage?
    - Which kind of plant had the most evidence of damage?
    - Did any sample plots have about the same number of damaged and undamaged plants?
    - How many sample plots had evidence of plant damage for five or more plants?
    - Which plants seem most at risk from plant predators?
    - Do you think the garden has a plant predator problem? Why or why not?

2. Ask older children:
    - How useful was this damage rating in assessing a predator problem?
    - How would you improve the method for rating damage?

Damage in the Garden	No Damage	Some Damage
Tomato	6	4
Corn	7	3
Bellpepper	1	9
Squash	5	5
Beans	3	7
Nasturtium	4	6
Mint	10	0

More Math in the Garden

Improving Your Damage Rating Method Create a more accurate method to rate damage to further identify degree of damage, such as adding lines or other colors to the red sticks to indicate little, medium, or lots of damage.

Mapping Damage Rate damage in different parts of the garden and map the location of plant predators and damage to identify "hot spots" of damage. Arrange to have the head of the garden join you to discuss options for controlling plant predators without the use of pesticides.

Guiding Others to Garden Predators Create an illustrated guide of garden pests and beneficial animals. Have youth gather information about animals that live in the garden.

Bud, Flower, Fruit Data

Ages 8-13

Youth observe and count the flowers, buds, and fruits on a stem of a plant. Then they count the number of stems on their plant. Using the data from one stem as a benchmark, they estimate the total number of flowers, buds, and fruits produced by their plant. These data are analyzed for the different stages of flowering to determine approximately how many flowers will be available to attract pollinators, which affects fruit production.

This activity introduces basic statistical skills — estimating, collecting, recording, organizing, computing, and interpreting data.

What You Need

For Each Team of Two or Three
- journals
- pencils and crayons

For the Group
- 2 databoards
  - "Flower Study Steps" chart
  - "Flower Data Chart"
- colored marking pens

Getting Ready

1. Locate an area of the garden where there are a number of plants in bloom. They can be the same or different kinds.

148
MATH IN THE GARDEN

The plants should be of a size that allows the youth to make their counts easily. Choose one plant to use in your demonstration of how to count buds, flowers, and fruit. Choose a plant with several stems and one with numerous buds, flowers, and fruits.

Sunflowers and other composite flowers like daisies contain many smaller flowers within the large blossom. Likewise, their mature heads contain many fruits. Tell your students that in this activity they should count each large blossom or "seed head" as one. At a later time, they may want to estimate the actual small flowers per blossom and fruits per seed head.

2. List the "Flower Study Steps" (page 151) on one databoard, and draw the "Flower Data Chart" (page 152) on the other.

3. If this is the first time youth have explored flowers, plan to use an illustration of a flower and a bee finger puppet to demonstrate pollination of a flower.

After flowering, the ovary surrounding fertilized eggs develops into the fruit. Sometimes a fruit is called a pod, especially if it has a thick skin, such as a pea pod.

Here We Go

1. Gather the youth around a flowering plant in the garden. Ask:
   ❦ What do you notice about flowers? [colors, smells, patterns]
   ❦ Why do you think animals such as bees visit flowers? [they are looking for nectar and pollen to eat]
   ❦ Why do you think plants need flowers? [Flowers attract pollinators so eggs can be fertilized and become seeds. Seeds grow into the next generation of the plant.]

2. Explain that flowers attract animals called pollinators. These animals transfer pollen between flowers. The pollen fertilizes the eggs in the ovary at the base of the flowers. Ask what pollinators the youth have seen in the garden. [hummingbirds, butterflies, moths, bees, beetles, bats, flies]

3. Announce that the youth will help find out how many flowers a plant produces to attract pollinators, and how many flowers in turn could develop into fruits. Pick several buds and fruits from your plant and have the youth figure out which is the bud. Pass the samples around, and encourage the youth to gently open them. Ask:
   ❦ What clues indicate a bud? [look for young petals and stamens]
   ❦ What clues indicate a fruit? [look for seeds inside]

bud

rose flower

fruit

MATH IN THE GARDEN

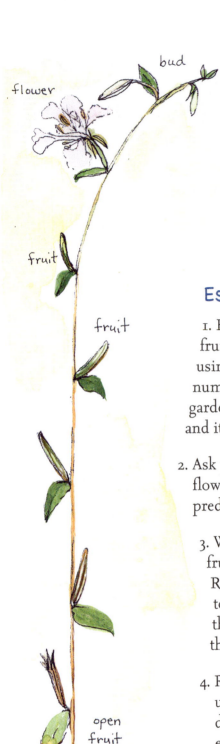

4. Ask volunteers to point out some buds on the plant. Ask:
   ❀ What do you think will happen to the bud when it gets older? [It grows into a full flower.]
   ❀ What do you think will happen if the flower is pollinated? [It will produce seeds and a fruit.]

5. Point out that farmers and gardeners can estimate their fruit crops based on the number of buds that can become flowers and the availability of pollinators to fertilize those flowers.

Estimating and Counting

1. Explain that rather than counting the number of flowers, buds, and fruits on the entire plant, you are going to get an estimated total by using the number counted on one stem and multiplying it by the total number of stems on the plant. Exact numbers are not needed because gardeners generally don't have the time to count every bud and flower, and it is not practical to do such a count.

2. Ask youth to predict how many of each of the flowering stages (bud, flower, and fruit) are on your demonstration plant. Record their predictions along the top of the "Flower Data Chart."

3. With volunteers, demonstrate how to count the flowers, buds, and fruits on a stem and record the numbers on the "Flower Data Chart." Refer to the "Flower Study Steps" as you proceed. Youth find it easier to count flowers starting at the bottom and moving up the stem. As they begin counting buds, have them check that the group agrees on the buds versus fruits.

4. Review the steps youth will use to collect data and determine the estimated totals. Have them make a chart in their journals with the same data columns used on the "Flower Data Chart."

Recording Flower Data

1. Divide the group into teams. Instruct them to choose a plant and write its name at the top of their data collection page. Before they begin collecting data, remind them to make a prediction of total number of fruits that might be produced by their chosen plant and record it in their journals. Also remind them to be gentle with the plants, and to work quietly so as not to scare away pollinators.

2. Circulate as teams observe and count flowers, buds, and fruits. Assist as necessary. Be sure they record results in their journals, including their predictions.

3. As teams complete their counts, have them record their data on the group "Flower Data Chart." When all teams are finished, gather the group and ask for their observations about the data collected from the single stem of their plants.

4. With everyone's help, use your demonstration plant data to show how to multiply the sum of flowers, buds, and fruits by the number of stems to determine an Estimated Total of flowers produced by this plant. Record this on the chart. Assist teams as they compute this total for their plants and record it on the "Flower Data Chart" and in their journals.

Analyzing Data and Determining Range and Mean

1. Stimulate discussion about the data and an understanding about the range of the data with the following kinds of questions:
   ❁ Which plant had the most buds? Which plant had the fewest buds? Tell the youth that the number of buds on the plants studied ranges from the least number to the greatest number. Record these numbers at the bottom of the chart, as illustrated on page 152. The difference between the two numbers is called the range. Calculate the range for buds and record it on the chart.

Range is the difference between the greatest number and the least number in a set of numbers.

Mean is the mathematical term for an average. To calculate a mean, the sum of two or more numbers is calculated and then divided by the number of addends.

MATH IN THE GARDEN

Flower Data Chart

Plants	Buds	Flowers	Fruits	Total/Stem (sum B+F+F)	# Stems	Estimated Total/Plant (Total/Stem × # Stems)
Sample	4	6	1	11	10	11 × 10 = 110
Sunflower	12	5	2	19	6	114
Tomato	15	6	0	21	9	189
Penstemon	3	15	8	26	3	78
Range of #s	3–15	5–15	0–8	11–26	3–10	78–189
Range	12	10	8	15	7	111
Mean	8.5	8	2.75	19.25	7	122.75

❁ Which plant had the most flowers? the fewest flowers? Determine the range and record it on the chart.

❁ What is the range for the number of fruits? The number of stems? Record the numbers and do the calculations as you did for buds and flowers.

2. Ask youth to compute the mean (average) number of buds on each stem. Review how to calculate the mean, and record it on the chart under Buds. For example: [(4+12+15+3)÷4=8.5] Repeat the computations for flowers, fruits, and number of stems. Record averages on the chart. See the databoard illustration, above.

3. As a group, determine the range and mean for the Estimated Total column. Record this data on the chart. Check for agreement in calculations.

4. Encourage youth to discuss their data by asking:
   ❁ How close were your predictions?
   ❁ How did making a prediction for the demonstration plant influence the predictions you made for your plant?
   ❁ How many total fruits do you estimate will be harvested from your plant?
   ❁ How did you determine your estimate?
   ❁ Who else might use estimated totals? [florist ordering roses]
   ❁ Who might want exact totals? [food service workers buying an apple for each child's snack]

More Math in the Garden

Examining Flower Parts Dissect different kinds of flowers to compare structures and numbers of flower parts.

Comparing Flower Cycles Compare the bud to fruit production in different kinds of plants.

Tracking Pollinators Observe pollinators in your garden to find out how many flowers they visit in a trip and which flowers they prefer.

Self-Similarity

Ages 8–13

In nature we sometimes find that a small part of an object resembles the whole. A little detail in the snowflake looks like a snowflake itself, and a twig often reminds us of the entire tree. This property is called "self-similarity" and is studied by mathematicians. In this activity youth learn to recognize self-similarity in plants, and to use simple mathematical rules to draw imaginary trees.

This activity explores pattern recognition and proportional reasoning, and introduces mathematical models to represent quantitative relationships.

What You Need

For Each Pair
- broccoli crown with stem
- journals
- pencils and crayons

For the Group
- broccoli crown with stem
- 2 databoards
  - "Self-Similarity" lineup
  - "Self-Similarity" chart
- colored marking pens

Getting Ready

1. Check the garden for availability of trees and bushes that exhibit self-similarity. The flowering tops of anise, yarrow, and elderbery exhibit self-similarity, and certain kinds of ferns are excellent.

2. Pick or purchase large broccoli stems that have not been trimmed back to the crowns. Following the activity, introduce youth to a nutritious snack of fresh broccoli florets and stem rounds.

MATH IN THE GARDEN

3. One one databoard make a "Self-Similarity" lineup (illustrated below) with title and levels on which you will lay broccoli branches in your demonstration. On the second databoard draw the "Self-Similarity" chart (see page 155).

4. Assemble the materials in an area where youth can sit with their partners during the introduction.

Here We Go

1. Introduce self-similarity using a large broccoli crown with stem. Point out how the broccoli has a thick stem that branches much like a tree. Each branch, with its smaller branches, also resembles a tree. This "tree within a tree" pattern is called self-similarity.

2. Explain that you are going to call the whole broccoli crown "Tree Level 1." Demonstrate how to break off a branch, and put the larger piece aside. Hold up the branch that is "Tree Level 2," and ask:
    ❋ If I break off another branch, what will the next level be?" [Level 3]
    ❋ How many levels do you predict you will find when you divide your own broccoli trees?

3. Give partners their broccoli, and ask them to predict the number of levels they will find. Working together they should remove a succession of smaller trees, always setting aside the larger tree and removing the next branch from the smaller one, until the remaining piece is too small to be further divided.

4. Tell the pairs to draw in their journals their lineup of broccoli trees from the largest level to the smallest and label each level. How many levels were they able to subdivide the broccoli?

Hunting for Self-Similarity in the Garden

1. Go for a self-similarity walk and have youth bring their journals and pencils. Gather around a tree or large bush to observe how branches divide into smaller ones. Have them follow the branching pattern to count how often it splits into smaller branches. After many such splits, the tree likely ends with leaves or flowers.

2. Suggest that youth use their fingers and thumbs to create an imaginary camera lens to frame and "photograph" a branch. As they focus on a branch, they can imagine it is a small tree hiding within a bigger tree. Give youth 10 minutes to sketch patterns of self-similarity that they detect in the plants and structures of the garden. Remind them to label where the pattern was found.

3. Depending on the numbers and ages of your participants, you may want to read the poem, Self-Similarity, as they stand observing the garden environment.

4. Invite the youth to think of other examples of self-similarity. [branching veins on an insect wing, branching blood vessels, branching coral, lightning, watershed patterns, fractals in geometry]

Making a Mathematical Tree

1. In your gathering place in the garden, demonstrate how to construct a mathematical tree using this rule: "Every branch ends with a fork of two branches."

Begin with a vertical line and add a fork of two branches at the top.

2. Write in the data for the first two levels and branch numbers on the "Self Similarity" chart.

3. Ask students to predict the number of branches for level three. Then draw the eight branches and add the number to the table. Ask them to predict the number of branches for a fourth level. (By now,

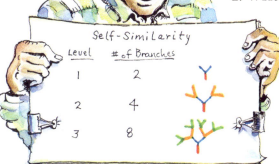

Self-Similarity
By Tim Aaronson

When a twig looks like a branch
and a branch looks like a tree,
you're looking at a case
of special symmetry.

If a branch looks like a twig,
but just not very big,
you are looking at a tree
with self-similarity.

A natural pattern lies
in your veins and arteries
and the wings of butterflies,
yes, self-similarity.

So when you find a tree
that's hiding in a branch,
and you find a branch
that's hiding in a twig,
do a little jig
for self-similarity!

youth are likely to have discovered that the number of branches doubles with each new level using the double-branch rule.)

4. Invite partners to generate their own mathematical trees using the double-branch rule in their journals. Remind them to make a table along the right side of the page and label the two columns at the top of the page to record the number of branches for each level. Encourage youth to continue drawing branches until they run out of room on the paper.

5. As you circulate among the partners, assist them in computing the branch numbers for the table. Show them that they can directly count, or add the branch number to itself. Encourage them to predict the next level before they attempt to count the new branches.

Comparing Mathematical Trees

1. Have the youth stand in a circle to display their mathematical trees. Ask guiding questions to stimulate a discussion of the drawings:
   * Why do all of these trees look so similar? [They used the two-branches rule.]
   * What are some of the differences between the trees? [Some people used short branches; some made long branches; some varied the branch length.]
   * What are some examples of other mathematical rules we could use for our tree? [Every branch has 3 branches coming off of it.]

2. Tell the group that there is an invisible part of the tree you want them to find, and to do so they should turn their drawings upside down. Ask what part of a tree grows downward like this? [Roots of most plants and trees grow downward and have a tree-like structure exhibiting self-similarity underground.]

More Math in the Garden

Making a Mathematical Garden Have youth draw a mathematical garden landscape using various patterns and rules of self-similarity.

Shadows — Change Over Time

Ages 8–13

This activity uses linear measurements and graphing to compare changes over time.

In this activity, youth determine firsthand how the height of a plant compares to the changing length of its shadow at various times during the day. It is amazing how fast a shadow length changes in the early morning and in the late afternoon hours. Shadows give youth data collection opportunities for tracking dynamic changes that can lead to new investigations of other changes.

What You Need

For the Group
- measuring tape
- small garden flags
- scissors
- roll of brightly colored string
- 2 databoards
    - "Plant & Shadow Lengths" table
    - "Shadow Length Over Time" graph
- colored marking pens

Getting Ready

1. Draw the "Plant & Shadow Lengths" table and the "Shadow Length Over Time" graph and put each on a databoard. See illustrations on page 159.

MATH IN THE GARDEN

157

2. Select a plant growing in a flat area that is not shaded by other plants or structures. Choose a plant that is no taller than the tallest child.

3. If you have only an hour to do this activity, it is best to do it before late morning or during mid-afternoon, when shadows change most rapidly. Shadows change the least at noon when the sun is directly overhead.

Here We Go

1. Gather the group out in the garden near the plant you plan to observe. Pose questions about shadows to see what the youth know and to reveal any misconceptions they may have. Ask:

A shadow is formed when any object is between a surface and a source of light. Sun shadows are formed by the earth's rotation as it travels around the sun. However, from our perspective on earth, it appears that the sun moves throughout the course of the day from sunrise to sunset.

- When have you seen shadows?
- What can create a shadow? [sun, light bulb, campfire, light shining on one side of an object]
- Will the shadow formed by a plant always be the same length? [No, the sun moves and the plant grows.]
- When do you think sun shadows are the longest? [early morning and late afternoon]
- How do you think the length of a plant's shadow is affected over the course of a day?
- How do you think the area of the plant's shadow is affected over the course of a day?

2. Tell the group that they will investigate how this plant's shadow changes over a period of time; explain the time frame.

3. Have two volunteers help you measure the height of the plant. Record the measurement and the date on the "Plant & Shadow Lengths" table. Ask a person to locate this plant height measurement on the y-axis of the "Shadow Length Over Time" graph and then to draw a horizontal line across the graph.

158

MATH IN THE GARDEN

4. Have a youth place a stake at the point on the shadow that is farthest from the plant. Measure the length of the shadow from the base of the plant to the stake. Record that measurement and time on the "Plant & Shadow Lengths" table. Ask:
   ❋ How can we determine if the point of the shadow farthest from the plant is created by the highest part of the plant? (Ask a volunteer to hold his hand in front of the top point on the plant. Have the children note where his hand's shadow appears on the plant shadow.)

5. Lay a brightly colored piece of string along the shadow's edge to outline it. Identify the space within it as the shadow of the plant.

6. Return to the plant in about 10 minutes and have the group make observations about its shadow. Ask:
   ❋ How has the shadow changed?
   ❋ Where is the farthest point on the shadow from the plant? Have a volunteer place another flag to mark that spot.

7. Take a new length measurement of the shadow and again record the measurement and the time it was taken on the table. Repeat at fairly frequent intervals until about 10 minutes before the youth leave.

Analyze the Shadow Data

1. Gather back at the plant. Look at the row of flags and the measurements recorded. Ask volunteers for observations about the data collected:
   ❋ How did the shadow's length change?
   ❋ When was the shadow length the longest? The shortest?
   ❋ How much did the shadow's length change in each time interval?
   ❋ Did the shadow's length change by the same amount in each interval?

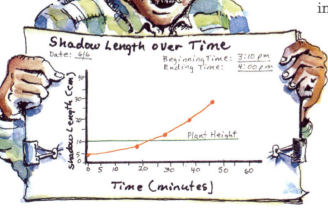

2. Show students how to graph the length of the shadow over time. Using a different colored pen than was used to indicate the plant's height, plot the first shadow length, then have volunteers plot the later shadow lengths in this same color. See illustration at left.

MATH IN THE GARDEN

3. Have a volunteer connect the points to see the trend of the shadow's change in length over time.
    - What does the graph tell us about the shadow's length during this time period?
    - If you were to measure the shadow over the next hour, how do you predict it would change?
    - What would a graph of the shadow of the plant over a 24-hour period look like?
    - What do you notice about the position of the flags in relation to each other?

- Do the flags make a curve or a straight line? [Flags make a curved line because they record the relative movement of the earth and sun during this time period.]

4. Invite the youth to compare the shape of the shadow now to the shape at the beginning of your observations. Remind them that the string outlined the shadow at the beginning. Ask:
    - How has the shadow changed?
    - What do you predict it will look like in 30 minutes?

More Math in the Garden

Observing the Shadow's Outline and Area Mark the shadow's outline at the beginning of your observations and at several intervals by laying colorful string around the shadow's perimeter (edge). Do this each time a new flag is placed at the top point of the shadow. Observe how the area shaded by the plant changes over time. Estimate the shadow's areas.

Temperatures inside Shadows Measure the temperature of the ground in the shade and in the sun. Discuss that some plants grow best in a lot of sun, some need part shade, and some need to be in the shade all the time. This may have to do with amount of light, temperature, and amount of moisture in the soil. Investigate which plants thrive in each of these environments.